MILESTONES TO MATURITY

Growing in the Laws of Grace

A Study of the Wilderness Books
(Exodus, Leviticus, Numbers, Deuteronomy)

Jack W. Hayford
with
Paul McGuire

THOMAS NELSON PUBLISHERS
Nashville

CONTENTS

Milestones to Maturity: Growing in the Laws of Grace (A Study of the Wilderness Books) is one of a series of study guides that focus exciting, discovery-geared coverage of Bible book and power themes—all prompting toward dynamic, Holy Spirit-filled living.

About the Executive Editor

JACK W. HAYFORD, noted pastor, teacher, writer, and composer, is the Executive Editor of the complete series, working with the publisher in the conceiving and developing of each of the books.

Dr. Hayford is Senior Pastor of The Church On The Way, the First Foursquare Church of Van Nuys, California. He and his wife, Anna, have four married children, all of whom are active in either pastoral ministry or vital church life. As General Editor of the *Spirit-Filled Life Bible*, Pastor Hayford led a four-year project, which has resulted in the availability of one of today's most practical and popular study Bibles. He is author of more than twenty books, including *A Passion for Fullness, The Beauty of Spiritual Language, Rebuilding the Real You,* and *Prayer Is Invading the Impossible.* His musical compositions number over four hundred songs, including the widely sung "Majesty."

About the Writer

PAUL McGUIRE is an author and speaker of increasing breadth of acceptance and demand, his ministry becoming noted for his spiritual sensitivity and forthrightness in addressing the New Age philosophy with practical and biblical wisdom. His local church and conference ministry effectively deals with pathways to restoring marriage, being healed from a broken past, and learning to minister to people in the New Age environment. His gift on these themes is enhanced by the way Paul confronts without condemning.

He was a student in Psychology at the University of Missouri, and he now lives in Santa Clarita, California with his wife, Kristina, and their three children: Paul (age 3) and twins Michael and Jennifer (age 1). The family is an active part of the congregation served by Dr. Hayford.

Paul McGuire's books include *Evangelizing the New Age, Supernatural Faith in the New Age, Marriage Breakthrough,* and *Healing from the Past.*

Of this contributor, the Executive Editor has remarked, "Paul is becoming a Holy Spirit instrument of pure and tender power in assisting victims in contemporary marital confusion and popularized error to come into spiritual liberty through Jesus Christ."

THE GIFT
THAT KEEPS ON GIVING

Who doesn't like presents? Whether they come wrapped in colorful paper and beautiful bows, or brown paper bags closed and tied at the top with old shoestring. Kids and adults of all ages love getting and opening presents.

But even this moment of surprise and pleasure can be marked by dread and fear. All it takes is for these words to appear: "Assembly Required. Instructions Enclosed." How we hate these words! They taunt us, tease us, beckon us to try to challenge them, all the while knowing that they have the upper hand. If we don't understand the instructions, or if we ignore them and try to put the gift together ourselves, more than likely we'll only assemble frustration and anger. What we felt about our great gift—all the joy, anticipation, and wonder—will vanish. And they will never return, at least not to that pristine state they had before we realized that *we* had to assemble our present with instructions *no consumer* will ever understand.

One of the most precious gifts God has given us is His Word, the Bible. Wrapped in the glory and sacrifice of His Son and delivered by the power and ministry of His Spirit, it is a treasured gift—one the family of God has preserved and protected for centuries as a family heirloom. It promises that it is the gift that keeps on giving, because the Giver it reveals is inexhaustible in His love and grace.

Tragically, though, fewer and fewer people, even those who number themselves among God's everlasting family, are opening this gift and seeking to understand what it's all about and how to use it. They often feel intimidated by it. It requires some assembly, and its instructions are hard to comprehend sometimes. How does the Bible fit together anyway?

What does Genesis have to do with Revelation? Who are Abraham and Moses, and what is their relationship to Jesus and Paul? And what about the works of the Law and the works of faith? What are they all about, and how do they fit together, if at all?

And what does this ancient Book have to say to us who are looking toward the twenty-first century? Will taking the time and energy to understand its instructions and to fit it all together really help you and me? Will it help us better understand who we are, what the future holds, how we can better live here and now? Will it really help us in our personal relationships, in our marriages and families, in our jobs? Can it give us more than just advice on how to handle crises? the death of a loved one? the financial fallout of losing a job? catastrophic illness? betrayal by a friend? the seduction of our values? the abuses of the heart and soul? Will it allay our fears and calm our restlessness and heal our wounds? Can it really get us in touch with the same power that gave birth to the universe? that parted the Red Sea? that raised Jesus from the stranglehold of the grave? Can we really find unconditional love, total forgiveness, and genuine healing in its pages?

Yes. Yes. Without a shred of doubt.

The *Spirit-Filled Life Bible Discovery Guide* series is designed to help you unwrap, assemble, and enjoy all God has for you in the pages of Scripture. It will focus your time and energy on the books of the Bible, the people and places they describe, and the themes and life applications that flow thick from its pages like honey oozing from a beehive.

So you can get the most out of God's Word, this series has a number of helpful features. Each study guide has no more than fourteen lessons, each arranged so you can plumb the depths or skim the surface, depending on your needs and interests.

The study guides also contain six major sections, each marked by a symbol and heading for easy identification.

 ## WORD WEALTH

The WORD WEALTH feature provides important definitions of key terms.

BEHIND THE SCENES

BEHIND THE SCENES supplies information about cultural beliefs and practices, doctrinal disputes, business trades, and the like, that illuminate Bible passages and teachings.

 AT A GLANCE

The AT A GLANCE feature uses maps and charts to identify places and simplify themes or positions.

 BIBLE EXTRA

Because this study guide focuses on a book of the Bible, you will find a BIBLE EXTRA feature that guides you into Bible dictionaries, Bible encyclopedias, and other resources that will enable you to glean more from the Bible's wealth if you want something extra.

 PROBING THE DEPTHS

Another feature, PROBING THE DEPTHS, will explain controversial issues raised by particular lessons and cite Bible passages and other sources to which you can turn to help you come to your own conclusions.

 FAITH ALIVE

Finally, each lesson contains a FAITH ALIVE feature. Here the focus is, So what? Given what the Bible says, what does it mean for my life? How can it impact my day-to-day needs, hurts, relationships, concerns, and whatever else is important to me? FAITH ALIVE will help you see and apply the practical relevance of God's literary gift.

As you'll see, these guides supply space for you to answer the study and life-application questions and exercises. You may, however, want to record all your answers, or just the overflow from your study or application, in a separate notebook or journal. This would be especially helpful if you think you'll dig into the BIBLE EXTRA features. Because the exercises in this feature are optional and can be expanded as far as you want to take them, we have not allowed writing space for them in this study guide. So you may want to have a notebook or journal handy for recording your discoveries while working through to this feature's riches.

The Bible study method used in this series revolves around four basic steps: observation, interpretation, correlation, and application. Observation answers the question, What does the text say? Interpretation deals with, What does the text mean?—not with what it means to you or me, but what it meant to its original readers. Correlation asks, What light do other Scripture passages shed on this text? And application, the goal of Bible study, poses the question, How should my life change in response to the Holy Spirit's teaching of this text?

If you have used a Bible much before, you know that it comes in a variety of translations and paraphrases. Although you can use any of them with profit as you work through the *Spirit-Filled Life Bible Discovery Guide* series, when Bible passages or words are cited, you will find they are from the New King James Version of the Bible. Using this translation with this series will make your study easier, but it's certainly not necessary.

The only resources you need to complete and apply these study guides are a heart and mind open to the Holy Spirit, a prayerful attitude, and a pencil and a Bible. Of course, you may draw upon other sources, such as commentaries, dictionaries, encyclopedias, atlases, and concordances, and you'll even find some optional exercises that will guide you into these sources. But these are extras, not necessities. These study guides are comprehensive enough to give you all you need to gain a good, basic understanding of the Bible book being covered and how you can apply its themes and counsel to your life.

A word of warning, though. By itself, Bible study will not transform your life. It will not give you power, peace, joy, comfort, hope, and a number of other gifts God longs for you to unwrap and enjoy. Through Bible study, you will grow in your understanding of the Lord, His kingdom and your place in it, and those things are essential. But you need more. You need to rely on the Holy Spirit to guide your study and your application of the Bible's truths. He, Jesus promised, was sent to teach us "all things" (John 14:26; cf. 1 Cor. 2:13). So as you use this series to guide you through Scripture, bathe your study time in prayer, asking the Spirit of God to illuminate the text, enlighten your mind, humble your will, and comfort your heart. He will never let you down.

My prayer and goal for you is that as you unwrap and begin to explore God's Book for living His way, the Holy Spirit will fill every fiber of your being with the joy and power God longs to give all His children. So read on. Be diligent. Stay open and submissive to Him. You will not be disappointed. He promises you!

Lesson 1/The Miraculous Deliverance of Israel

The late science fiction writer, Robert A. Heinlein, wrote the classic novel *Stranger in a Strange Land*. It is about a man from Mars who found himself living in a strange culture called Planet Earth. In a similar manner, believers in Jesus Christ, who are citizens of heaven, have been called to live here as aliens and sojourners on this planet until we arrive at our final destination, which is the kingdom of heaven.

Just as the ancient nation of Israel lived in relationship to the personal living God of the universe among a pagan culture that viewed them as somewhat strange, so we, too, as the people of God, must live in a culture that is often hostile to our beliefs and practices. In fact, the individual Christian experience is parallel to the journey that Israel took through the wilderness as recorded in Exodus, Leviticus, Numbers, and Deuteronomy. Each of us who has accepted Jesus Christ as his Lord and Savior understands the journey from slavery to freedom in the Promised Land that God leads us into. What the children of Israel experienced in their journey toward freedom has much to share with us as modern believers.

In *Milestones to Maturity: Growing in the Laws of Grace*, we will explore the powerful truths that the children of Israel learned while following the God of redemption. The Pentateuch's books of Exodus, Leviticus, Numbers, and Deuteronomy contain such a rich wealth of information that it would take volumes just to begin to understand the depth and breadth of Israel's experience with God. Obviously, time and space do not permit an exhaustive undertaking here. For those interested in further study, I suggest books, such as Lawrence O. Richards's *Complete Bible Handbook* (Word Books, 1982); Bruce Wilkinson's and Kenneth Boa's *Talk Through the Bible* (Thomas Nelson Publishers, 1983); Warren Wiersbe's *With the Word* (Oliver Nelson, 1991); James E. Smith's *The Pentateuch, a Survey* (Restoration Press, 1989); Herbert Lockyer's *All the Miracles of the Bible* (Zondervan, 1961).

The thrust of the book *Milestones to Maturity: Growing in the Laws of Grace* is to help you understand some of the key spiritual truths that God was teaching His people as He led them from slavery to the Promised Land. These truths are the "milestones to maturity" that enabled the people of God to "grow in the laws of grace." Likewise, as our Lord and Savior Jesus Christ leads us out from the bondage and slavery of sin into His Promised Land, He teaches us spiritual keys to victory through the Holy Spirit and the Word of God. Exodus, Leviticus, Numbers, and Deuteronomy are Old Testament books that are literally bursting with applicable truths that can help our daily lives. Studying these books is like walking through a gold mine that is rich in gold: everywhere you look you can see precious nuggets and streaks of glowing gold.

As much as possible this study guide focuses on what the Bible actually says and is not an interpretation. In each scripture verse there is a wealth of information. Before you read *Milestones to Maturity,* I encourage you to spend time in prayer to God, asking Him to use this study guide to affect your life powerfully through the truth of God's Word contained in it. The key to appreciating the Wilderness Books is in seeing within God's teachings to Israel those living truths that the Holy Spirit can apply to our lives today.

As we open our eyes to these truths, we allow the Lord to do the kind of inner work that will release us to move from slavery at any point in our lives to real victory in Him.

INTRODUCTION

The Book of Exodus, the second book of the Pentateuch, continues the Genesis account, which deals with how a small family of seventy people became a mighty nation of millions. The Hebrew nation lived in almost constant slavery for 430 years. Exodus is the historical account of Moses, a type of Christ, who leads the people out of bondage in Egypt. The Exodus account includes how God supernaturally delivered His people out of bondage and their subsequent journey from Egypt to Sinai where they received God's Law and instructions on how to build an earthly tabernacle for God. The story of Israel's journey of deliverance from slavery under Pharaoh to the Promised Land is a type of how Jesus Christ saves the Christian from the bondage of sin. In addition, the Christian is freed from slavery under Satan in the world system and is led by Jesus Christ supernaturally to the Promised Land or the kingdom of heaven.

First Corinthians 10:11 says, "Now all these things happened to them as examples, and they were written for our admonition, upon whom the ends of the ages have come." The key truth here is that the truths found in Exodus, Leviticus, Numbers, and Deuteronomy are not written just for historical understanding. They contain powerful spiritual truths for us as believers today. Jesus Christ delivers us from the power of sin and leads us into the kingdom of heaven. Although our final destination is a very real place called heaven, where we will live eternally with God, kingdom living begins here on earth as we walk in the power of the Holy Spirit and appropriate kingdom principles in our lives. The story of Israel's journey out of slavery in Egypt to the Promised Land contains numerous truths regarding our personal spiritual journey out of slavery under Satan to freedom under the lordship of Christ.

Before we go further, read Exodus 1:1—13:16, which details the account of the miraculous deliverance of Israel. Taking the one hour required to comprehensively overview this pivotal event will be worth the time as we progress. Go ahead; do it now!

ISRAEL'S SUFFERING IN EGYPT: A PEOPLE UNDER BONDAGE AND IN SLAVERY (Exodus 1:1–22)

Here we see that God is a covenant-keeping God. We read in Exodus 1:7, "But the children of Israel were fruitful and increased abundantly, multiplied and grew exceedingly mighty; and the land was filled with them." God kept His covenant (or agreement) that He made with Abraham when he was ninety-nine years old. Read Genesis 17:1–5 and apply the promise God made to Abraham then to what was happening in Exodus 1:7.

Describe how God's covenant promise to Abraham was fulfilled in Exodus 1:7.

In Genesis 1:28 we read, "Then God blessed them, and God said to them, 'Be fruitful and multiply; fill the earth and subdue it; have dominion over the fish of the sea, over the birds of the air, and over every living thing that moves on the earth.'" These were God's instructions to Adam and Eve before the Fall of Man in the Garden of Eden. God is a God of fruitfulness, multiplication, and dominion. This is an important principle to comprehend. The Fall of Man produced a loss of fruitfulness, multiplication, and dominion. We read the account of God's redemption of mankind from the slavery of sin through the blood of the covenant, which has its full expression in the blood of the Lamb—Jesus Christ. We see that God is restoring to man the dominion, fruitfulness, and multiplication that he lost through disobedience of God's Word.

 BIBLE EXTRA

In Deuteronomy 28 we read specifically how God promises to reestablish fruitfulness, dominion, and multiplication in the lives of His people. The lesson to learn here is that when we obey God's covenant we should expect fruitfulness, multiplication, and dominion at every dimension of life. In John 10:10 we read, "The thief does not come except to steal, and to kill, and to destroy. I have come that they might have life, and that they may have *it* more abundantly."

God's plan for man is always abundance and increase. However, since the Fall of Man in the Garden, shortages, lack, poverty, infertility, and loss abound due to the entrance of sin into the human race. Egypt is a type of our present world system. Pharaoh is a type of Satan whom the Bible calls the "god of this age." This present world system is not God's plan for mankind. It is a fallen world that is polluted with sin. Leviticus 25:23 says, "The land shall not be sold permanently, for the land *is* Mine: for you *are* strangers and sojourners with Me." In other words, we are just passing through this life. This world in its present fallen state is not our real home. The apostle John reminds us, "For all that *is* in the world—the lust of the flesh, the lust of the eyes, and the pride of life—is not of the Father but is of the world. And the world is passing away, and the lust of it; but he who does the will of God abides forever" (1 John 2:16, 17).

In light of 1 John 2:16, 17, what is our relationship to be with this present world system? How does it parallel the children of Israel's experience in Egypt ?

Pharaoh is a type of Satan, and this present world system is to Christians like Egypt was to the children of Israel. Pharaoh set "taskmasters" over the children of Israel to afflict them. In Exodus 1:11 we read, "Therefore they set taskmasters over them to afflict them with their burdens. And they built for Pharaoh supply cities, Pithom and Raamses." As in ancient Egypt, this present world system is a slave planet for God's people. Although we may have temporary pleasures and God's blessings in this world, we must remember that this present world system is not our real home. God gives us a promise of deliverance and freedom.

BIBLE EXTRA

Satan attempts to set "taskmasters" over God's people so that he can afflict them with burdens. These "taskmasters" may be people or situations. However, behind these "taskmasters" are very real principalities and powers (Eph. 6:12) who are attempting to afflict God's people with burdens. In Jesus Christ, God has a specific plan of deliverance for His people. It is not God's will that His people have brutal "taskmasters" over them. God is a covenant-keeping God. He has a plan of freedom for us if we will obey Him and have complete faith in His Word.

In Acts 10:38 we read, "How God anointed Jesus of Nazareth with the Holy Spirit and with power, who went about doing good and healing all who were oppressed by the devil, for God was with Him." Pharaoh oppressed the children of Israel in Egypt by afflicting them. Similarly, Satan oppresses people today under the present world system. However, Jesus Christ heals all those who are "oppressed by the devil."

List ways that you have had "taskmasters" afflict you or the people you know. Learn to recognize that behind these people or situations there is often a real "taskmaster," Satan, who is attempting to destroy you or limit your effectiveness in life.

Moses is a deliverer and a type of Jesus Christ. God, who is the covenant-keeping God, sent Moses as a deliverer for His people in the midst of their oppression in Egypt. In the same way, Jesus Christ is a deliverer for God's people in the midst of oppression in this present world system. God is a God of love. Since the Fall of Man in the Garden of Eden, God has been in the business of rescuing and saving humankind.

MOSES AS A TYPE OF CHRIST
(Exodus 2:1—4:31)

When Moses was born, Pharaoh had ordered the firstborn boys of all the children of Israel killed (Ex. 1:16). When Jesus Christ was born, King Herod had ordered that all male children of Israel under two years old be killed (Matt. 2:16). In this way, Moses was a type of Christ; and in both instances,

Satan was using men in an effort to stop God's method of salvation for His people.

Many would see our modern-day abortion holocaust as Satan's attempt at destroying the possibilities that God might have in the lives of the unborn. Remember, in Genesis 1:28 we find that God is a God of fruitfulness and multiplication. Satan hates fruitfulness and multiplication. He attempts to abort both human lives and the dreams inside men and women. Look up John 10:10. What does this passage of Scripture tell us about the Adversary?

Clearly, Satan's perverted nature is the exact opposite of God's nature. While God desires increase, multiplication, and abundance, Satan thrives on stealing, killing, and destruction. In distinct contrast to Satan, Jesus Christ came to give us the abundant life.

How does the murder of the young male children of Israel in both Pharaoh's and Herod's times reveal the heart of Satan?

What is the difference between Satan's plan for our lives and God's plan for our lives?

Exodus 3:3–20 tells the story of God's call on Moses' life. What does Exodus 3:11 tell us about Moses' response?

Many of us, when we hear God's call on our lives for ministry or to accomplish a specific assignment, shrink back in fear. One reason we do this is that as we look at our own human resources, we feel inadequate to complete the task. Instead of looking to ourselves, we should be focusing on the supernatural resources God makes available to us when He calls us to do something. Like Moses, we make the mistake of saying, "Who *am* I?" instead of acknowledging with the apostle Paul:

> That the God of our Lord Jesus Christ, the Father of glory, may give to you the spirit of wisdom and revelation in the knowledge of Him, the eyes of your understanding being enlightened; that you may know what is the hope of His calling, what are the riches of the glory of His inheritance in the saints, and what *is* the exceeding greatness of His power toward us who believe, according to the working of His mighty power. (Eph. 1:17–19)

What highlights about God's purpose in you do you find in Ephesians 1:17–19?

When God calls us to do something, He wants us to understand that it is by His resources, not ours, that it will get done. From your own life experience, write down things that God has called you to do and how He has miraculously supplied the resources you need.

In Exodus 3:9–15 we read how God is a covenant-keeping God. Note in verse 15 that God calls Himself the

"God of Abraham, the God of Isaac, and the God of Jacob."
In relationship to the fact that God is a covenant-keeping God,
why does He give Himself this name?

In Exodus 3:7 we read, "And the LORD said: 'I have
surely seen the oppression of My people who *are* in Egypt, and
have heard their cry because of their taskmasters, for I know
their sorrows.'" Here we discover that God is infinitely com-
passionate and loving. He truly cares about the needs and pain
of His people.

WORD WEALTH

Know, *yada.* To know, to perceive, to distinguish, to
recognize, to acknowledge, to be acquainted with; in a few
instances to "know intimately," that is, sexually; also to
acknowledge, recognize, esteem, and endorse.[1]

In Matthew 10:30, 31 Jesus Christ tells His disciples,
"But the very hairs of your head are all numbered. Do not fear
therefore; you are of more value than many sparrows." In the
previous passages, Jesus Christ was telling them that not even a
sparrow falls to the ground without the Father's will. He was
teaching them the tremendous compassion and care that a loving Heavenly Father has for His people. Just as God knows the
number of hairs upon our head, He also knows about our sorrows. This is very difficult for us to comprehend. In our
human understanding, we cannot fathom how a God so big

who runs the entire universe would be that intimately concerned about our lives or our sorrows. Yet the Bible says that God is love, and one of the aspects of this divine love is that God is intimately concerned with the lives of His people.

In Exodus 4:1–9 God promises to use miraculous signs in front of Pharaoh and the people of Egypt. God is a supernatural God, and He sometimes chooses to speak through signs and wonders.

What kind of supernatural signs did God use in each of the following passages?

Ex. 4:1–17

2 Cor. 12:12

Heb. 2:4

When God calls a man to ministry, how will He supernaturally fit him to fulfill that call?

In Exodus 4:1–9 how did God move Moses from the place of saying "Who *am* I?" to the position of supernatural authority and recognizing that his sufficiency was in God and not of himself?

GOD'S COVENANT-KEEPING PROMISE OF DELIVERANCE COMES TRUE
(Exodus 5:1—11:10)

In Exodus 5:1–21 we see that the taskmaster increases the oppression. The taskmasters force the children of Israel to fulfill their daily quota in building bricks even after they take the straw away from them. Dr. Jack Hayford calls this the "treadmill experience." They are working harder and actually going nowhere. Satan establishes "treadmill experiences" in the lives of believers. However, God is a covenant-keeping God, and He promises them deliverance. The *Spirit-Filled Life Bible* describes a covenant as an agreement between two parties. Usually one party was superior to the other. It contained permanent pledges made to each other, ratified by a ritual or a ceremony, such as circumcision.

Read Genesis 17:1–11. How did the covenant that God made with Abraham apply to Exodus 6?

Exodus 5:13, 14 illustrates the "treadmill experience." Describe the "treadmill experience" in your own words.

In Exodus 5:21 we see the children of Israel reacting in fear instead of faith to their situation. God had sent them a deliverer, and as soon as things got rough they began to complain. Why were they angry at Moses and Aaron?

Exodus 6:2–8 records God's strong promise to deliver the children of Israel as He swore in His covenant. In Exodus 6:3 the words "God Almighty" are used to translate from the Hebrew *El-Shaddai,* that is, "The God Who Is Enough," "The All-Powerful" and "The One Who Is Self-Sufficient," which showed that God was the source of all blessing.[2]

Write down how God is *El-Shaddai* in your life as you face battles and have needs.

Even though God promised this tremendous deliverance, the Hebrew slaves did not believe God's word of deliverance. In his Bible study *Learning How to Live Again,* Dr. Jack Hayford explains that a key in the deliverance of the slaves was learning how to get rid of the slave mentality, which they had developed during their years of servitude. This slave mentality can be found in the lives of believers in Jesus Christ. In Matthew 13:58 we read, "Now He did not do many mighty works there because of their unbelief." A slave mind-set that says, "It's too good to be true," as well as cynicism and doubt, can lock out the possibility of God's miraculous provision.

In Exodus 7:3–5 God tells Moses and Aaron that He is going to perform signs and wonders so that the Egyptians will know that He is Lord. Review the following passages and identify the ten plagues God brought on Pharaoh and his people.

1. 7:20

2. 8:6

3. 8:17

4. 8:24

5. 9:6

6. 9:10

7. 9:23

8. 10:13

9. 10:22

10. 12:29

The final visitation of God, the death of the firstborn, demonstrates to the Egyptians that He is the Lord of life and death. Their false god Osiris was proven to be impotent as a giver of life in the face of Yahweh's judgment. God shows signs and wonders in the land of Egypt so that the Egyptians might know that He is Lord. God speaks to people through signs and wonders on a personal basis and on a national scale. In Ezekiel 38:23 and in John 11:47, we see God working signs and wonders for the purpose of calling people to Himself.

 AT A GLANCE

The Ten Plagues on Egypt[3]	
The Plague	**The Effect**
1. Blood (7:20)	Pharaoh hardened (7:22)
2. Frogs (8:6)	Pharaoh begs relief, promises freedom (8:8), but is hardened (8:15)
3. Lice (8:17)	Pharaoh hardened (8:19)
4. Flies (8:24)	Pharaoh bargains (8:28), but is hardened (8:32)
5. Livestock diseased (9:6)	Pharaoh hardened (9:7)
6. Boils (9:10)	Pharaoh hardened (9:12)
7. Hail (9:23)	Pharaoh begs relief (9:27), promises freedom (9:28), but is hardened (9:35)
8. Locusts (10:13)	Pharaoh bargains (10:11), begs relief (10:17), but is hardened (10:20)
9. Darkness (10:22)	Pharaoh bargains (10:24), but is hardened (10:27)
10. Death of firstborn (12:29)	Pharaoh and Egyptians beg Israel to leave Egypt (12:31–33)
God multiplied His signs and wonders in the land of Egypt that the Egyptians might know that He is the Lord.	

THE EXODUS
(Exodus 12:1—13:16)

FAITH ALIVE

Read Exodus 12:1–51 and Luke 22:14–20. The original Passover was a feast that celebrated the deliverance of the children of Israel because of their covenant with God. When they placed the blood of a lamb on their doorposts the death plague passed over their homes. This foreshadowed the work of Jesus Christ, who is the true Passover Lamb of God. When we accept Jesus Christ into our lives by faith and are washed clean from our sins by the blood of the Lamb, we can live forever with God in Paradise. The deathforce of sin is broken and we have eternal life in Christ.

In Luke 22:14–20 how is the New Covenant promise for the believer in Jesus Christ similar to the deliverance promised by Moses in the Old Testament? Apply this truth to your own life.

1. *Spirit-Filled Life Bible* (Nashville, TN: Thomas Nelson Publishers, 1991), 89, "Word Wealth: 3:7 know."
2. Ibid., 91, note on 6:3.
3. Ibid., 92, Chart: "The Ten Plagues on Egypt."

Lesson 2/The Miraculous Journey to Sinai
(Ex. 13:17—18:27)

In Exodus 13:17—18:27, we read of the miraculous journey of the children of Israel to Mount Sinai and God's supernatural deliverance of Israel from Pharaoh's oppressive hand. In order to understand how these truths apply to our lives today we need to recognize the *slave mentality* that had rooted itself in the minds of the children of Israel. Because the children of Israel still saw themselves as slaves rather than as the real people of God which the covenant declared they were, they actually inhibited what God was trying to do in their lives.

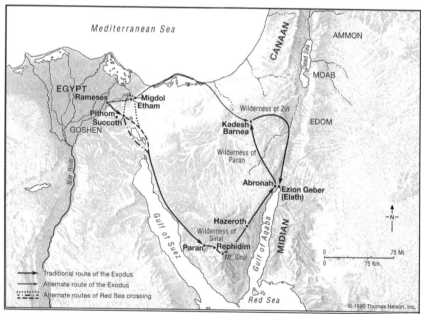

The Exodus from Egypt. Note that this map shows the site from which the waters of the Red Sea have receded.[1]

It is important to understand that, in order to fully move into the flow of what God has for us, we must throw off the fears of the "old man" and the *slave mentality* and boldly follow God into the Promised Land. God continually gave the Israelites supernatural provisions, divine healing, victory in warfare, and other blessings that were contingent on their learning to stop complaining and to begin renouncing their *slave mentality.* It was as they learned to live before their God in praise, worship, and faith in His promises, that the kingdom blessings began to flow into their lives.

SUPERNATURAL DELIVERANCE AT THE RED SEA
(Exodus 13:17—15:21)

Exodus 14:4 states that God supernaturally hardened Pharaoh's heart so that the Egyptians would know that He is Lord. Proverbs 21:1 teaches us that the king's heart is in the "hand of the Lord." Sometimes we will see obstacles in our life that are divinely ordained.

When we pray for God's guidance and commit our ways to the Lord, then we can be confident that even doors that are shut may be God's leading or timing. List five doors that were shut in your life.

1.

2.

3.

4.

5.

As you look back, you can be thankful that God did not open that door even though it may have been painful at the time.

In Exodus 14:12, 13 we read, "*Is* this not the word that we told you in Egypt, saying, 'Let us alone that we may serve the Egyptians'? For *it would have been* better for us to serve the Egyptians than that we should die in the wilderness. And Moses said to the people, 'Do not be afraid. Stand still, and see the salvation of the LORD, which He will accomplish for you today. For the Egyptians whom you see today, you shall see again no more forever.'"

Verse 12 reveals the *slave mentality* in the minds of the children of Israel. Even as the process of divine deliverance was under way, they complained and actually longed to return to slavery rather than have to develop faith and trust in God, which would bring them true freedom. In your own words, explain why the children of Israel wanted to return to Egypt. Explain how this principle applies to your walk with Christ.

Verse 13 reveals a powerful lesson in trusting God. Write down what that lesson is.

Exodus 14:21 gives the account of Moses exercising supernatural authority. How does this compare with the lesson that Jesus Christ taught His disciples in Mark 11:23, 24?

Exodus 14:31 tells us that in the face of an awesome miracle Israel temporarily believed the Lord and feared Him. What lesson does this teach us for our own lives?

Exodus 15:1–19 teaches us a principle of praise and worship. The "Song of Moses" shows us the importance of singing a "new song" to the Lord. How can we apply this principle of praise and worship in our daily lives?

GOD'S SUPERNATURAL PROVISION AND SUPPLY
(Exodus 15:22—17:7)

Exodus 15:26 reveals to us God's provision of divine healing. "If you diligently heed the voice of the LORD your God and do what is right in His sight, give ear to His commandments and keep all His statutes, I will put none of the diseases on you which I have brought on the Egyptians. For I *am* the LORD who heals you."

WORD WEALTH

Heals, *rapha'*. To cure, heal, repair, mend, restore health. Its participial form *rophe'*, "one who heals," is the Hebrew word for doctor. The main idea of the verb *rapha'* is physical healing. Some have tried to explain away the biblical teaching of divine healing, but all can see that this verse speaks of physical diseases and their divine cure. The first mention of the word *rapha'* in the Bible (Gen. 20:17) refers unquestionably to the cure of a physical condition, as do references to healing from leprosy and boils (Lev. 13:18; 14:3).[2]

PROBING THE DEPTHS

Although some try to do away with the clear biblical teaching concerning divine healing, it is a truth that is taught in both the Old and New Testaments. Look up the following scriptures and write down how these verses make reference to the biblical truth concerning divine healing.

Luke 18:35–43

Acts 10:38

Acts 19:12

In Exodus 16:1–20, God gave the children of Israel manna for food. Likewise, God provides "daily bread" for His children today.

Read Exodus 16:1–20. In verses 2 and 3 we see that the children of Israel complained against Moses and Aaron. How does the fact of their complaining indicate that they still had the slave mentality?

Notice the word "complaints" (sometimes translated "murmurings" or "grumblings") in verses 2, 8, and 12. What is the lesson to us in those verses?

Exodus 16:23–30 teaches us the principle of the Sabbath rest. This illustrates that it is God who is our Source and not our "hard work." The world teaches us that we can only "get" through hard work. The Bible does not minimize the importance of hard work. However, God tells us that He will provide for us when we rest and observe the Sabbath. What can happen to us if we violate God's command to obey a Sabbath?

What does Romans 14:5, 6 say to us about the Sabbath?

In Exodus 17:1–7, Moses strikes the rock and gets water from the rock to quench the thirst of the children of Israel. How does this compare with John 7:37, 38 where Jesus said, "If anyone thirsts, let him come to Me and drink. He who believes in Me, as the Scripture has said, out of his heart will flow rivers of living water"?

Read 1 Corinthians 10:4, and explain the relationship between that verse and Exodus 17:1–7.

VICTORY OVER THE AMALEKITES
(Exodus 17:8–16)

Exodus 17:11 illustrates the principle that our primary warfare is spiritual and not physical. Our victory is in Jesus Christ and not in our own strength. Exodus 17:11 states, "And so it was, when Moses held up his hand, that Israel prevailed: and when he let down his hand, Amalek prevailed."

The idea here is that God gave Israel victory, and their victory was not based on their military might. In verse 15 it says, "And Moses built an altar and called its name, The-LORD-Is-My-Banner." This term comes from the Hebrew *YAHWEH NISSI*. The *Spirit-Filled Life Bible* defines the biblical word "banner" as a polelike standard beneath which the armies or communities rallied. When lifted up, it called the people together for battle.[3]

Zechariah 4:6b says, "'Not by might nor by power, but by My Spirit,' says the LORD of hosts." What principle is revealed in both Exodus 17:11 and Zechariah 4:6?

In Exodus 18:1–27, the principle of delegating authority is established. Elders are appointed to share in godly leadership. What principle can we learn from this chapter about leadership and management?

1. *Spirit-Filled Life Bible* (Nashville, TN: Thomas Nelson Publishers, 1991), map on 102.

2. Ibid., 105, "Word Wealth: 15:26 heals."

3. Ibid., 108, note on 17:15.

Lesson 3/The Miraculous Revelations at Sinai (Ex. 19:1—40:38)

Exodus 19:1—40:38 deals with the miraculous revelations to the children of Israel at Sinai. First, God appears to them as the covenant-keeping God and gives them the Ten Commandments as part of this covenant. These Ten Commandments are intended to enhance rather than to restrict their life-style. In them, God was trying to give His people the spiritual foundation for real freedom and the highest quality of life. Some Christians still view God's rules and requirements as restrictive and burdensome. Yet the Ten Commandments, along with all of God's laws, are actually commandments for life and maximum possibility. Far from being restrictive, all of God's laws are power lines of real spiritual and psychological freedom that produce purpose, power, and fulfillment in the lives of people who choose to obey them.

Unfortunately, our world conveys the idea that people who have conservative religious beliefs are somehow missing out on all the fun. In reality, nothing could be further from the truth. It is only those who are not slaves to their passions and momentary whims who are truly free to enjoy life.

GOD'S APPEARING AT SINAI
(Exodus 19:1–25)

In Exodus 19:3–6, God tells Moses to tell the people that, if they keep His covenant, they will be a special treasure to Him above all the people of the earth—"a kingdom of priests and a holy nation." Dr. Jack Hayford writes, "In these verses, the Lord indicates His objective for His delivered people. His purpose for their destiny requires their understanding His essential priority for them: worship—His redemptive goal and kingdom reinstatement. As they learn to worship as a nation of priests, they will discover His foundational means for possessing their future victories (as ones whose domain, or 'kingdom,' He has promised). Their restored kingdom rule, from sharing to 'kingdom' possession, extends from their walk before God in worship."[1]

How does verse 6 and the principle of our being a kingdom of priests apply to our walk with Christ today?

THE TEN COMMANDMENTS
(Exodus 20:1–21)

The Ten Commandments are not given as a set of restricting instructions. Instead, they are liberating guidelines designed with man's maximum fulfillment in mind. As we look at the following commandments, we should ask the question, How does obeying this commandment keep me or society free? The key is to view the Ten Commandments as the powerful, life-enhancing guidelines they are, and not as a restrictive or life-inhibiting set of orders. Read verses 3–17 and write down each of the Ten Commandments described in these verses:

1.

2.

3.

4.

5.

6.

7.

8.

9.

10.

In verse 3 it says, "You shall have no other gods before Me." How does obeying this commandment keep an individual or a nation free?

Verse 8 says, "Remember the Sabbath day, to keep it holy." How does adherence to this commandment keep an individual psychologically, spiritually, and physically rested?

In verse 12 the Lord says, "Honor your father and your mother, that your days may be long upon the land which the LORD your God is giving you." How can we apply that in our own lives?

In verse 14 the Lord tells us, "You shall not commit adultery." How does obeying this commandment assure us of total psychological, spiritual, and physical fulfillment?

In verse 17 we read, "You shall not covet your neighbor's house; you shall not covet your neighbor's wife, nor his male servant, nor his female servant, nor his ox, nor his donkey, nor anything that *is* your neighbor's." This commandment strikes right at the heart of American society's belief of "new," "better," and "more." What is God trying to teach us in this commandment?

THE BOOK OF THE COVENANT
(Exodus 20:22—23:19)

This section explains in detail how the Ten Commandments are to be lived out in society in practical terms. The Ten Commandments are to have a spiritual, psychological, physical, sociological, and political effect in a nation.

In Exodus 22:18–25, the Law deals with very specific issues. For instance, verse 18 states, "You shall not permit a sorceress to live." The *Spirit-Filled Life Bible* defines sorcery as "trying to force a deity or spirits to do the bidding of the sorcerer."[2] This would also include the contemporary occult practice of channeling. In my book, *Evangelizing the New Age*, the term "channeling" is defined as "what the Old Testament termed mediumship, consulting with spirits, and spiritism. Channeling or mediumship is when an individual willfully yields to a spirit by going into a trancelike state."[3]

Read Leviticus 19:31; 20:6, 27; Deuteronomy 18:10, 11; 1 Samuel 28:3–10; Jeremiah 27:9, 10 to further grasp this issue of sorcery and occult practices from the biblical perspective. Then answer the question, What was the reason for the apparent harshness of the commandment in Exodus 22:18?

Verse 19 talks about bestiality. What does God call this sin in Leviticus 18:23?

What was to be done with those who violated this command? Why? (Lev. 20:15, 16)

Finally, besides the obvious spiritual and moral reasons for this commandment, how does it affect man biologically? What does sex with an animal say about the violation of the sacredness of human sexuality within marriage?

Exodus 22:21 talks about illegal aliens and immigrants. As Christians, what should be our attitude and behavior toward people who have come to our nation for freedom?

Verse 25 discusses principles of banking and lending money to God's people who are poor. What does this say about charging excessive interest to poor people in order to make a profit? (Lev. 25:35–38)

GOD'S ANGEL OF PROTECTION
(Exodus 23:20–33)

Exodus 23:20–33 talks about God's Angel of protection. God gave the children of Israel a fantastic promise that He would send His Angel to guide them and protect them. Verse 20 states, "Behold, I send you an Angel before you to keep you in the way and to bring you into the place which I have prepared." Hebrews 1:14 specifically talks about the angels: "Are they not all ministering spirits sent forth to minister for those who will inherit salvation?"

   WORD WEALTH

Angel, *mal'ach.* A messenger, ambassador; someone dispatched to do a task or relay a message; specifically an "angel" or heavenly messenger from the Lord. Found more than 200 times, *mal'ach* is usually translated "angel" (though often translated "messengers" when referring to human messengers; see Gen. 32:3; 1 Sam. 16:19; 2 Kin. 7:15). Angels, mentioned extensively in the Old Testament, were sent to assist or inform the patriarchs, Balaam, David, the prophet Zechariah, and others. Not all angels are of the "angelic" sort; see Proverbs 16:14 (which might have been translated "death angels"); Psalm 78:49; Proverbs 17:11. Psalm 104:4 portrays the supernatural qualities (spirit, fire) of the Lord's messengers.[4]

Believers in Jesus Christ have angels assigned to protect them today. We can be confident that God protects and guides His people with guardian angels. In any situation in which we find ourselves, God has an angel there to protect us. Psalm 91:11, 12 says, "For He shall give His angels charge over you, to keep you in all your ways. In *their* hands they shall bear you up, lest you dash your foot against a stone." Dr. Billy Graham suggests that each believer must have at least two guardian angels assigned to protect them.

How should the fact that we have angels assigned to protect us give us confidence in life?

How is this theme developed in 2 Kings 6:16, 17?

A very important theme is developed in the Bible concerning angels. We are not alone. God has an army to defend us that is very real in the invisible realm.

In Exodus 23:22, there is a condition to God's using His Angel to drive out the enemies of the children of Israel. What is the condition?

Exodus 23:25 states, "So you shall serve the LORD your God, and He will bless your bread and your water. And I will take sickness away from the midst of you." How does this promise apply to us today?

In verse 27 we read, "I will send My fear before you, I will cause confusion among all the people to whom you come, and will make all your enemies turn *their* backs to you." How do the verses 28–30 apply to our lives?

In verses 32 and 33 there is a condition to God's protection. Explain briefly what this condition is.

THE COVENANT IS UNDERSTOOD
(Exodus 24:1–18)

In Exodus 24 Moses read the Book of the Covenant to all the people. Verse 7 records that the people responded by saying, "All that the LORD has said we will do, and be obedient." The people were well aware that they were entering into a divine contract with God. If they obeyed the covenant, things would go well for them. If they disobeyed, then things would go badly for them. It was not complicated. It was very simple.

In Exodus 24:16, 17 God's glory rested on Mount Sinai. In verse 17 we read, "The sight of the glory of the LORD *was* like a consuming fire on top of the mountain in the eyes of the children of Israel." In applying these truths to our lives, we must understand that there have been times when we have seen God's glory in our lives. It may have not been in a physical manifestation, yet God's glory was there. What were the children of Israel supposed to learn? What are we supposed to learn from seeing God's glory?

DIRECTIONS CONCERNING THE TABERNACLE
(Exodus 25:1—31:18)

Specific directions were given in the construction of a tabernacle or tent where God's presence would dwell (Ex. 25:9). How do you think the earthly tabernacle of God compares with 1 Corinthians 3:16, which states, "Do you not know that you are the temple of God and *that* the Spirit of God dwells in you?"

In terms of its purpose as a dwelling place for God's presence?

In terms of its requirements for keeping the "pattern"? (Ex. 25:9)

In terms of the use of the temple for the people's worship?

AT A GLANCE

ISRAEL'S OTHER SACRED TIMES[5]	
Sabbath	Every seventh day was a solemn rest from all work.
Ex. 20:8–11; 31:12–17; Lev. 23:3; Deut. 5:12–15	
Sabbath Year	Every seventh year was designated a "year of release" to allow the land to lie fallow.
Ex. 23:10, 11; Lev. 25:1–7	
Year of Jubilee	The 50th year, which followed seven Sabbath years, was to proclaim liberty to those who were servants because of debt, and to return lands to their former owners.
Lev. 25:8–55; 27:17–24; Ezek. 46:17	
The New Moon	The first day of the Hebrew 29 or 30-day month was a day of rest, special sacrifices, and the blowing of trumpets.
Num. 28:11–15; Ps. 81:3	
Dedication (Lights or *Hanukkah*)	An eight-day feast in the ninth month (Chislev) commemorating the cleansing of the temple from defilement by Syria, and its rededication.
John 10:22	
Purim (Lots)	A feast on the 14th and 15th of the 12th month (Adar). The name comes from Babylonian *Pur*, meaning "Lot."
Esth. 9:18–32	

The ark was a chest that was a symbol of God's presence (Ex. 25:10). The *Spirit-Filled Life Bible* describes the ark as a chest about 3-3/4 feet long and 2-1/4 feet wide and high. It was a symbol of God's presence, the place where He would meet and speak with Moses (v. 22).[6]

Exodus 25:17 reveals the mercy seat or the atonement cover. It was a symbol of God's eternal throne. The priests sprinkled blood on and in front of the mercy seat, symbolizing the blood of Jesus Christ giving us access to the throne of God. How does Hebrews 9:1–28 reveal this truth?

The cherubim were angelic beings associated with the guarding and bearing of God's throne. Read Revelation 4:1–11 and contrast this with Exodus 25:18.

The table of showbread served as a symbol of God who is the provider of food (Ex. 25:23). In John 6:48 Jesus Christ says that He is "the bread of life." How is the showbread a type of Christ?

The lampstand served as a symbol of God who is the light for the children of Israel (Ex. 25:31–40). Jesus Christ is the light of the world (John 8:12). What is the relationship between these two scriptures?

Exodus 26:31–34 refers to the veil. The Most Holy or the Holy of Holies was the place behind the inner veil. Matthew 27:51 talks about the veil of the temple being ripped in two by

Jesus Christ when He died on the cross. How has the death of Jesus Christ as the complete eternal sacrifice made it possible for believers to enter into the presence of God through the blood of the Lamb?

AT A GLANCE

THE PLAN OF THE TABERNACLE[7]

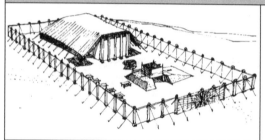

The tabernacle was to provide a place where God might dwell among His people. The term *tabernacle* sometimes refers to the tent, including the holy place and the Most Holy, which was covered with embroidered curtains. But in other places it refers to the entire complex, including the curtained court in which the tent stood.

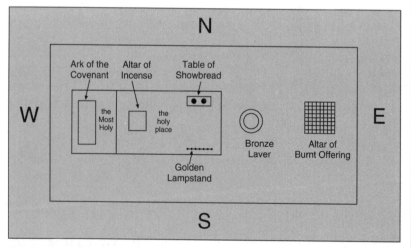

N

Ark of the Covenant   Altar of Incense   Table of Showbread

W   the Most Holy   the holy place   Bronze Laver   Altar of Burnt Offering   E

Golden Lampstand

S

This illustration shows the relative positions of the tabernacle furniture used in Israelite worship. The tabernacle is enlarged for clarity. See also Chart: The Furniture of the Tabernacle, p. 48.

How is the altar a type of the cross of Jesus Christ when Jesus was the sacrificial Lamb of God? (Ex. 27:1)

Exodus 27:9–19 tells about the court around the tabernacle. What activities took place in the court of the tabernacle?

Exodus 27:20 gives instructions for the care of the lampstand. The oil of the lampstand was a type of the Holy Spirit burning in the lives of believers. How does Matthew 25:1–13 admonish us as believers to allow the light of God's Spirit to burn brightly in us until Christ returns?

The ephod was a four-piece, vestlike garment through which Aaron symbolically bore Israel on his shoulders in God's presence (Ex. 28:5–14). The breastplate was a single piece of fabric with twelve stones, like the ephod, which symbolized the twelve tribes of Israel that Aaron bore in the presence of God (Ex. 28:15–30).

The words HOLINESS TO THE LORD were engraved on a special plate worn by Aaron on his turban. In order for the priest to go into the presence of the Lord, he had to be completely holy. How can we be completely holy and enter into the presence of God?

The sin offering or the guilt offering was offered for intentional or unintentional sins (Ex. 29:10–14). The guilt for the wrongdoing was symbolically transferred to an animal through the laying on of hands. How is Jesus Christ our sin offering?

IDOLATRY AND THE GOLDEN CALF
(Exodus 32:1–35)

Man's propensity for sin, even after great revelation, is revealed in Exodus 32. Is it possible that, even after we have received Jesus Christ into our lives, we can still have idols in our hearts?

Write down some possible idols that we could have in the secret chambers of our hearts, idols that we need forgiveness for worshiping.

What does it mean to be under the lordship of Christ?

How does Moses play the role of an intercessor, standing in the gap for the children of Israel? God spares the children of Israel judgment because of His covenant with them.

REPENTANCE AND RENEWAL OF THE COVENANT
(Exodus 33:1—35:3)

God promises to give Israel His presence. God's presence comes with His rest. Exodus 33:14 says, "And He said, 'My Presence will go *with you,* and I will give you rest.'"

    WORD WEALTH

Give rest, *nu'ach.* To rest, settle down; to be soothed or quieted; to be secure; to be still; to dwell peacefully. This verb occurs about sixty-five times, first in Genesis 8:4, which states that the ark rested on the mountains of Ararat. *Nu'ach* is the verb that describes the Spirit of God upon the Messiah (Is. 11:2), or upon the seventy elders of Israel (Num. 11:25). The name "Noah" ("Rest-Giver," or "Comforter") is derived from *nu'ach.* In the present reference, God's presence will give rest to His people, that is, His presence soothes, comforts, settles, consoles, and quiets us.[8]

The key lesson here for us as believers is to make sure that God's presence is with us and that we do not depart out of the presence of God. As Christians who have received the Holy Spirit we need to walk and dwell in the presence of God.

God grants Moses' request to see His glory (Ex. 33:18–23). However, Moses is only allowed to see God from the back. In addition, Moses had to be protected by a rock in order to see God's glory. God's glory is so intense that it is only in Jesus Christ, the Rock of our salvation, that we can behold God's glory. Psalm 24:8 says, "Who *is* the King of glory? The

LORD strong and mighty, the LORD mighty in battle." If we allow Him, God's glory will fight our battles for us. How do we make sure that the glory of the Lord goes before us?

Exodus 34:1–35 describes the renewal of the covenant. Specifically, how does God renew the covenant with Israel?

Verse 1 instructs Moses to make new tablets. What role do the commandments play in God's covenant?

God's glory literally illuminated Moses' face (Ex.34:29, 30, 33–35). In the same way, the glory of God and the power of the Holy Spirit affect our countenance. How can we make sure the glory of the Lord radiates from our lives as we walk with Him?

Read 2 Corinthians 3:12–18. How is the veil taken away in Christ?

THE BUILDING OF THE TABERNACLE
(Exodus 35:4—40:33)

The tabernacle is constructed according to God's directions to Moses.

How is the tabernacle financed? (Ex. 35:4–9, 20–29)

How were the articles in the tabernacle made? (Ex. 35:10)

How do Exodus 35:30–35 and Exodus 36:1 reveal that God divinely equips people with wisdom, skill, and anointing by His Spirit?

What confidence can we have when we need a special anointing of wisdom as these men did? (James 1:5)

THE FURNITURE OF THE TABERNACLE[9]

Ark of the Covenant
(Ex. 25:10–22)
The ark was most sacred of all the furniture in the tabernacle. Here the Hebrews kept a copy of the Ten Commandments, which summarized the whole covenant.

Bronze Laver
(Ex. 30:17–21)
It was to the laver of bronze that the priests would come for cleansing. They must be pure to enter the presence of God.

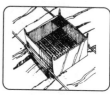

Altar of Burnt Offering
(Ex. 27:1–8)
Animal sacrifices were offered on this altar, located in the court in front of the tabernacle. The blood of the sacrifice was sprinkled on the four horns of the altar.

Gold Lampstand
(Ex. 25:31–40)
The gold lampstand stood in the holy place, opposite the table of showbread. It held seven lamps, flat bowls in which a wick lay with one end in the oil of the bowl and the lighted end hanging out.

Table of Showbread
(Ex. 25:23–30)
The table of showbread was a stand on which the offerings were placed. Always in God's presence on the table were the 12 loaves of bread representing the 12 tribes.

Altar of Incense
(Ex. 30:1–10)
The altar of incense inside the tabernacle was much smaller than the altar of burnt offering outside. The incense burned on the altar was a perfume of a sweet-smelling aroma.

THE GLORY OF THE LORD FILLING THE TABERNACLE
(Exodus 40:34–38)

Exodus 40:34–38 describes the preparations for the tabernacle that would allow the glory of the Lord to fill the tabernacle. Exodus 40:34 states, "Then the cloud covered the tabernacle of meeting, and the glory of the LORD filled the tabernacle."

Again, an important truth for us is that we are to be holy as individuals so that the glory of the Lord can fill us as people. We become holy, not through a rigorous program of self-effort, but rather through being cleansed by the blood of Jesus Christ and allowing His righteousness to purify us.

The central message of the Book of Exodus is that God is personally present in the midst of His people. Exodus 40:37, 38 says, "But if the cloud was not taken up, then they did not journey till the day that it was taken up. For the cloud of the LORD *was* above the tabernacle by day, and fire was over it by night, in the sight of all the house of Israel, throughout all their journeys."

God does not lead us today by a cloud by day and a fire by night. However, He does guide us with His presence. How can we be led by the Holy Spirit today? Does God lead us with the same measure of precision with which He led Israel?

In Acts 10:9–16 and 11:4–18 how does God lead Peter by the Holy Spirit?

Read Acts 27:21–24 and describe how Paul knew what the outcome of the journey would bring.

Look up Isaiah 30:21 and write down how we can be led by the Spirit of God today.

AT A GLANCE

TRUTH-IN-ACTION through EXODUS[10]
Letting the LIFE of the Holy Spirit Bring Faith's Works Alive in You!

Truth Exodus Teaches	Text	Action Exodus Invites
1 Four Keys to Understanding God Successful Christian living begins with knowing who God is. In Ex., God reveals part of His nature and character. Knowing God in truth will affect our behavior. Ex. gives four keys to make our lives more faithful and fruitful.	3:14, 15	**Understand** that God is! His Name is "I AM WHO I AM." **Rest** on this foundation. **Be grounded** and established in Him.
	15:25, 26	**Receive** God as "The Lord Who Heals You." To heal is His nature; His will is to make us whole.
	17:15	**Rely upon** God who is "The Lord Your Banner." As you surrender to Him—your Victory, Miracle, and Protection—your battle against the flesh will succeed.
	31:13	**Pursue** God who is "The Lord Who Makes You Holy." His life in us makes our holiness possible.
2 Steps to Holiness God calls us to be holy, "set apart to Him and His purposes." God intends His people to be distinguished in nature and in character from the world—different in the way we think, act, and live. This difference will be visible and bring God glory.	7:1—11:10	**Know** that God deals differently with us than with the world (see 8:23; 9:26; 10:23; 11:7).
	12:7	**Rely** on the blood of Jesus to protect you from all evil (see 1 Pet. 1:18, 19).
	19:5	**Obey** God's Word and you will become His "special treasure."
	21:5	**Be Jesus' bondslave.** He will open your ears to hear His voice clearly and understand His Word.
	32:26–29	**Be zealous** for God's holiness. He honors those who honor Him.
3 Guidelines to Godly Living Godly living is living with God in your life and His Life in you. He gives guidelines to help us build our lives on His precepts. God calls us to acts of faith that build godliness. Without faith, our acts become vain religion. Godliness embraces godly practice and shuns vain religious acts.	3:3	**Stay alert** to **seek** out God's working. It often comes in a way we do not expect.
	12:15, 19, 20; 13:3, 6, 7	**Participate** regularly in the Lord's Supper to share in His deliverance and life.
	14:13, 14	**Be still** as God works. You will see His deliverance.
	16:4	**Be careful** to apply God's Word. He wants us to follow His instructions.

	23:16; 34:22 25:8; 33:15 31:12–17; 33:14	**Celebrate** God's blessings. **Dwell in** and **esteem** God's Presence. It distinguishes us from everyone else. **Rest** in God's Sabbath. His rest gives us rest from our own works (see Heb. 4:10, 11).
4 **Keys to Wise Living** God calls His people to wisdom. Wisdom is knowing how to apply truth. Ex. gives principles that teach us how to live wisely and please God. It also teaches us certain wise practices. The Holy Spirit will train us to practice wisdom as a discipline that will lead to the fullness of life.	19:8; 24:3, 7 20:1–17 20:20 23:2, 3 23:15 32:1 35:30–35	**Do not trust** yourself to obey God's Word. Depend upon His Holy Spirit. **Meditate** on the Ten Commandments regularly to learn God's moral nature and character. **Learn** reverence for the Lord; it will keep you from sinning. **Suspect** majority opinion that proposes deviance. Evil is often popular but disobeys God. **Give** every time you gather with God's people for worship. It shows faith that He provides for you. **Do not become impatient** with God. It leads to sin. **Recognize** that any skill or ability you have is God's gift. **Be grateful** for His gifts, avoiding pride.
5 **Keys to Understanding Authority** God rules His people through delegated authority. All authority is from God (see Rom. 13). To distrust those He places over us is to distrust Him. God calls His people to a submissive attitude toward His leaders. He cautions us to be careful how we speak about them.	16:8; 22:28 22:18 35:20–29	**Do not grumble** against spiritual leadership. You thus grumble against the Lord and rebel. **Avoid** and **shun** the occult. To seek out spiritual direction from evil leads to death. **Listen** to those God sends to speak to and lead us. **Do not rebel** against their leadership. To disregard godly leaders is to disregard Him.

1. *Spirit-Filled Life Bible* (Nashville, TN: Thomas Nelson Publishers, 1991), 110, "Kingdom Dynamics: A Kingdom of Priests."

2. Ibid., 114, note on 22:18.

3. From *Evangelizing the New Age* © 1989 by Paul McGuire, 44. Published by Servant Publications, P.O. Box 8617, Ann Arbor, Michigan 48107. Used with Permission.

4. *Spirit-Filled Life Bible*, 647, "Word Wealth: 32:21 angel."

5. Ibid., 180, Chart: "Israel's Other Sacred Times."

6. Ibid., 118, note on 25:10.

7. Ibid., 120, "The Plan of the Tabernacle."

8. Ibid., 131, "Word Wealth: 33:14 give rest."

9. Ibid., 137, Chart: "The Furniture of the Tabernacle."

10. Ibid., 143–144, "Truth-in-Action through Exodus."

Lesson 4/Leviticus—the Sacrificial System
(Lev. 1:1—7:38)

Tradition says that the Book of Leviticus was written by Moses around 1445 B.C. Leviticus focuses on holiness as it applies to ordinary life. Crucial to the understanding of the Book of Leviticus is that holiness is not some abstract theological concept, but an actual foundation for the power of God's presence at work in the life of an individual or nation. The word "holy" appears more than eighty times in the book.

The call of God in the Book of Leviticus is for the people of God to be holy and pure before God. In the Old Testament, the sacrificial system was instituted for the sins of the people and pointed the way to Jesus Christ as the ultimate sacrifice for sin. In both cases, God made provision for the sins of the people through the blood covenant. The good news is that, even if God's people miss the mark and sin, they can be made holy through the blood of the Lamb, which is Jesus Christ. Therefore, holiness and purity before God are not unattainable for the contemporary believer in Jesus Christ. It is the blood that cleanses us from all sin and makes us holy before a holy God. We can have confidence before God because Jesus Christ has made atonement for our sins.

THE BURNT OFFERING
(Leviticus 1:1–17)

What was the purpose of the burnt offering or sacrifice that was offered twice daily? (v. 4)

John 1:29, says, "The next day John saw Jesus coming toward him, and said, 'Behold! The Lamb of God who takes away the sin of the world!'" How is Jesus Christ the true burnt offering?

THE GRAIN OFFERING
(Leviticus 2:1–16)

Everything we own and the entire created universe belongs to God. We simply borrow and are stewards of the resources that God has entrusted us with. Even our children, wives, and husbands belong to the Lord. In fact, our own bodies, spirits, and souls belong to the Lord. Therefore, the popular notion that we own our own bodies or even our own lives is purely contrived. What two powerful spiritual principles are taught by the grain offering?

Action (2:1)

Attitude (2:13)

Read Romans 12:1, 2 and Hebrews 13:15, 16 and describe how the grain offering foreshadowed the Christian's giving himself in daily sacrifice to God through Jesus Christ.

THE PEACE OFFERING
(Leviticus 3:1–17)

A peace offering was an optional sacrifice, which could be brought in conjunction with a confession or a vow or simply as a freewill offering of gratitude (7:11–21). It consisted of a sacrificial animal, of which part was burned, part was eaten by the priests, and part was returned to the worshiper to eat. It was a festive offering, foreshadowing the New Testament Communion meal as well as any other festive Christian meal commemorating salvation.[1]

What was the purpose of the peace offering?

Why was the offering to be without blemish or imperfection? (v. 1)

THE SIN OFFERING
(Leviticus 4:1—5:13)

The sin offering foreshadowed purification from sin's pollution by the blood of Jesus Christ. In The New Testament, it is the responsibility of every believer in Jesus Christ to regularly examine himself or herself and ask God for forgiveness from sin so that we can be purified from sin's pollution in our lives. In 1 John 1:7–9 we read, "But if we walk in the light as He is in the light, we have fellowship with one another, and the blood of Jesus Christ His Son cleanses us from all sin. If we say that we have no sin, we deceive ourselves, and the truth is not in us. If we confess our sins, He is faithful and just to forgive us *our* sins and to cleanse us from all unrighteousness."

In the Old Testament, the children of Israel gave an actual sin offering for purification from sin. How can we apply the truth of Jesus Christ's being our sin offering in our own personal lives? What does 1 John 1:7–9 teach us?

THE TRESPASS OFFERING
(Leviticus 5:14—6:7)

Leviticus 5:14—6:7 warns us about the casual use of our tongue in either swearing falsely or speaking thoughtlessly. In our culture, a loose tongue is commonplace. However, believers in Jesus Christ are to recognize the power of the spoken word.

     FAITH ALIVE

James 3:1–12 gives us further instructions on the use of our tongues. Verse 2 reminds us, "For we all stumble in many things. If anyone does not stumble in word, he is a perfect man, able also to bridle the whole body."

God considered the power of the tongue of such importance in the Old Testament that a trespass offering had to be given for speaking thoughtlessly (Lev. 5:4). Jesus Christ had some very strong words to say about the words we speak: "But I say to you that for every idle word men may speak, they will give account of it in the day of judgment. For by your words you will be justified, and by your words you will be condemned" (Matt. 12:36, 37).

How can our words free people or put them in bondage?

How is God going to hold us responsible for the words we speak to people?

How can you see that your words may have the power to release people to be everything they were created to be through your way of expressing yourself?

Our words are very powerful and can build or destroy lives. This is why God views our words with such high priority. Our words can build up or tear down individual lives, marriages, communities, and nations. How should that affect what we say? How can we be sure we use our tongues wisely?

How did the trespass offering require restitution? (Lev. 5:16)

OTHER INSTRUCTIONS
(Leviticus 6:8—7:38)

Leviticus 6:12, 13 states, "And the fire on the altar shall be kept burning on it; it shall not be put out. And the priest shall burn wood on it every morning, and lay the burnt offering in order on it; and he shall burn on it the fat of the peace offerings. **A fire shall always be burning on the altar; it shall never go out.**"

What lesson regarding our devotion and zeal to the Lord can be found in verse 13? How does this compare with Revelation 3:16?

1. *Spirit-Filled Life Bible* (Nashville, TN: Thomas Nelson Publishers, 1991), 149, note on 3:1.

Lesson 5/Priestly Service in the Sanctuary
(Lev. 8:1–36)

AARON AND SONS TAKE SPIRITUAL LEADERSHIP
(Leviticus 8:1–36)

In Leviticus 8:2 we read, "Take Aaron and his sons with him, and the garments, the anointing oil, a bull as the sin offering, two rams, and a basket of unleavened bread." In Leviticus 8:12 Moses anointed Aaron: "And he poured some of the anointing oil on Aaron's head and anointed him, to consecrate him." The anointing set Aaron apart for leadership and in the service of priestly worship. In the Old Testament, both kings and priests were anointed to serve as God's leaders.

In 1 John 2:20 we read, "But you have an anointing from the Holy One, and you know all things." According to this verse, every believer has an anointing from the Holy One. How does this anointing set us apart as believers in Jesus Christ who live in the midst of a spiritually dark culture?

 FAITH ALIVE

On page 6 of the January/February 1993 issue of *The Foursquare World Advance,* "Anointed for Battle," evangelist Reinhard Bonnke declares that, throughout history, each generation has been uniquely anointed for battle against the enemy of our souls. In the Old Testament, Moses anointed

Aaron for service. Today, believers in Jesus Christ have the opportunity of being anointed by Jesus Christ. However, Bonnke urges us to remember that God has not given bows and arrows to us to act as ornaments. He knows the enemy is facing us and we must face the enemy.

Just as Aaron was anointed for specific service, we as believers in Jesus Christ have been anointed to face the Adversary. In your own words, explain briefly the specific reasons why God has anointed you.

GOD CONFIRMS SPIRITUAL LEADERSHIP
(Leviticus 9:1–24)

In Leviticus 9:22–24, we see Aaron and Moses blessing the people. "Then Aaron lifted his hand toward the people, blessed them, and came down from offering the sin offering, the burnt offering, and peace offerings. And Moses and Aaron went into the tabernacle of meeting, and came out and blessed the people. Then the glory of the LORD appeared to all the people."

Here we see that Moses and Aaron blessed the people. It is important that we understand that blessing involves far more than saying "God bless you!" when someone sneezes. God has given every believer in Jesus Christ the power to bless others with supernatural authority. When Moses and Aaron blessed the people, the glory of the Lord appeared to the people.

Proverbs 31:28 says, "Her children rise up and call her blessed." The following "Word Wealth" gives us further understanding of the word *blessed*.

    WORD WEALTH

Blessed, *'ashar.* Happy, blessed, prosperous, successful, straight, right, contented.[1]

In Matthew 5:3 Jesus Christ said, "Blessed *are* the poor in spirit, for theirs is the kingdom of heaven." This New Testament word comes from the Greek word *makarios* and suggests a happy condition in which congratulations are in order. Believers in Jesus Christ have the supernatural authority to bless people. By taking action and blessing people, believers in Jesus Christ release God's favor, protection, resources, and goodness in people's lives. Blessing is a tangible force of God's goodness activated in people's lives. It is a release of kingdom authority. In Genesis 12:2 the Lord said to Abraham, "I will make you a great nation; I will bless you and make your name great; and you shall be a blessing. I will bless those who bless you, and I will curse him who curses you; and in you all the families of the earth shall be blessed."

 WORD WEALTH

"In [Gen. 12:2] God promises to make Abraham great, and God did bless Abraham in many ways, including material blessing. . . . In Galatians 3:13, 14, God promises to give all believers the blessing of Abraham, telling us that Jesus became a curse for us so that we might receive 'the blessing of Abraham.' This begins, of course, with our being born-again, or becoming new creatures in Christ Jesus. But 'the blessings of Abraham' involve other things as well. The Lord wants us to prosper—spiritually, emotionally, physically, and materially."[2]

As believers in Jesus Christ, how can we release the power of blessing in the lives of others and of our families?

What specific results can we expect when we pray for blessing?

After Moses and Aaron blessed the people, we read in Leviticus 9:24, "And fire came out from before the LORD and consumed the burnt offering and the fat on the altar. When all the people saw *it*, they shouted and fell on their faces." God is holy, and the purity of His presence manifests itself in fire. On the Day of Pentecost, God poured out tongues of fire on believers. The fire of the Holy Spirit is a real manifestation of God's presence. "Then there appeared to them divided tongues, as of fire, and *one* sat upon each of them" (Acts 2:3).

When God's glory was poured out in the New Testament upon believers on the Day of Pentecost, what two things happened? (Acts 2:4)

THE PRICE OF DISOBEDIENCE
(Leviticus 9:1–24)

Leviticus 10:1 tells us that Nadab and Abihu offered "profane fire before the LORD." Profane fire was a form of idolatrous worship. Jewish tradition also teaches that Nadab and Abihu were intoxicated in the presence of the Lord. Leviticus 10:3 warns us that God is holy, yet these men trifled in the presence of the Lord. The result was that "fire went out from the LORD and devoured them" (v. 2). Then God spoke through Moses saying, "By those who come near Me I must be regarded as holy; and before all the people I must be glorified" (v. 3).

They were specifically warned, "Do not drink wine or any intoxicating drink, you, nor your sons with you, when you go into the tabernacle of meeting, lest you die. *It shall be* a statute forever throughout your generations, that you may distinguish between holy and unholy, and between unclean and clean" (Lev. 10:9, 10). Clearly, the use of intoxicating beverages was forbidden to the priests who were supposed to come near God.

Why was this commandment given? (vv. 10, 11)

What warning does this give to us as we desire to draw near to the presence of God?

In our time, there have been more serious examples of trifling in the presence of God. A few ministers and ministries have attempted to hide immorality or offer profane fire and have suffered God's judgment. It is not that God does not forgive. He certainly does. However, God's power and presence are very holy. In our morally relativistic culture, the truth of God's holiness is not easily understood. God's power cannot be played with lightly. God's presence can send revival and healing as well as judgment. Yet when men play with the presence of God and trifle with God's awesome power, the real danger of destruction exists, stemming from the holiness of God.

As a believer in Jesus Christ, I welcome in the presence of God through the blood of Jesus Christ. Yet I must not take this privilege lightly. How can I be sure that I do not offer *profane fire* or idolatrous worship as they did in Leviticus 10:2?

THE SIN OF ELEAZAR AND ITHAMAR
(Leviticus 10:12–20)

Who were Eleazar and Ithamar? (v. 12)

What had Moses commanded them and Aaron to do?

In Leviticus 10:17–19, Moses inquired why the sin offering was not eaten in the holy place. What response was given in verse 19 that satisfied Moses and why?

FAITH ALIVE

Three key truths are revealed in Leviticus 8:1—10:20. These truths are:

* **Anointing** (8:1, 2)

* **Blessing** (9:22, 23)

* **The Purifying Fire of God's Holiness** (9:24)

The lesson here is that God desires to anoint and bless us. However, through disobedience of His Word and making wrong choices, we can block the flow of this anointing and blessing. The key is to allow our hearts to be freshly rekindled with the purifying fire of God's presence on a daily basis. When the fire of God's presence burns within us, it consumes any residual idolatry in our hearts and creates in us a holiness and a passion for Him that allows God's anointing and blessing to flow.

1. *Spirit-Filled Life Bible* (Nashville, TN: Thomas Nelson Publishers, 1991), 924, "Word Wealth: 31:28 blessed."
2. Ibid., 22, "Kingdom Dynamics: God's Heart to Prosper His People."

Lesson 6/The Laws of Impurities
(Lev. 11:1—16:34)

ANIMAL IMPURITIES
(Leviticus 11:1–47)

The people were set apart in a holy relationship with the living God. Certain foods were prohibited to eat. In addition, the Hebrew dietary laws had health benefits that are just being discovered today by modern nutritional research. The contemporary Jewish religious culture still honors these dietary laws by having *kosher* foods and *kosher* restaurants, which offer only foods that the Law allows.

The lesson being taught in Leviticus 11:1–47 is that God was creating a holy community. Holiness required "a conscious awareness of the divine presence in daily living, including foods which are acceptable to be eaten."[1]

CHILDBIRTH IMPURITIES
(Leviticus 12:1–8)

In natural life, the Hebrews were taught the difference between clean and unclean. After a woman had borne a child, she had to be purified and an offering had to be made (v. 2).

Male children had to be circumcised (v. 3). Circumcision was a physical sign of being set apart from the other nations of the earth whose male populations were not circumcised. In the New Testament, we read in Romans 2:29, "But *he is* a Jew who *is one* inwardly; and circumcision *is that* of the heart, in the Spirit, not in the letter; whose praise *is* not from men but from God."

What does it mean to be circumcised in the heart?

How do we allow the Holy Spirit to circumcise our hearts?

SKIN IMPURITIES
(Leviticus 13:1—14:57)

 BEHIND THE SCENES

The Book of Leviticus teaches the relationship between physical wholeness and holiness. Critics of the Bible claim that Scripture is unscientific, yet Leviticus reveals that the Israelites understood that germs and microscopic viruses could be transmitted through physical contact. In it the plague of leprosy is dealt with through the very strictest of hygienic requirements.

DISCHARGE IMPURITIES
(Leviticus 15:1–33)

Again, levitical laws were centuries ahead of modern medicine. The transmission of AIDS and other sexual diseases occurs through the discharge of bodily fluids. The levitical laws were designed to stop the transmission of disease through bodily discharges. Leviticus 15:16–27 deals specifically with discharges or bodily fluids related to the sexual organs.

When God made commandments against adultery, sex outside of marriage, homosexuality, and even bestiality, He did so with the full knowledge that certain sexual practices were destructive to an individual's spiritual, psychological, physical, and genetic make-up.

MORAL IMPURITIES
(Leviticus 16:1–34)

Moral sins and impurities were to be dealt with through the sacrifice of an animal. Leviticus 16:8 talks about a *scapegoat's* being used as a means of atonement. "Then Aaron shall cast lots for the two goats: one lot for the LORD and the other lot for the scapegoat."

In verses 21 and 22 we read, "Aaron shall lay both his hands on the head of the live goat, confess over it all the iniquities of the children of Israel, and all their transgressions, concerning all their sins, putting them on the head of the goat, and shall send *it* away into the wilderness by the hand of a suitable man. The goat shall bear on itself all their iniquities to an uninhabited land; and he shall release the goat in the wilderness."

The sins of the nation were temporarily removed through the sacrifice of the scapegoat. The ceremony prefigured the crucifixion of Jesus Christ on the cross.

Read Hebrews 9 and compare it with Leviticus 16:1–34.

Hebrews 9:11, 12 states, "But Christ came *as* High Priest of the good things to come, with the greater and more perfect tabernacle not made with hands, that is, not of this creation. Not with the blood of goats and calves, but with His own blood He entered the Most Holy Place once for all, having obtained eternal redemption." Explain how Jesus Christ is the final and complete sacrifice or the ultimate "scapegoat" for the sins of the human race.

1. *Spirit-Filled Life Bible* (Nashville, TN: Thomas Nelson Publishers, 1991), 159, note on 11:2.

Lesson 7/The Holiness Code
(Lev. 17:1—26:46)

SACRIFICES TO DEMONS
(Leviticus 17:1–16)

Leviticus 17:7 reads, "They shall no more offer their sacrifices to demons, after whom they have played the harlot. This shall be a statute forever for them throughout their generations." This verse warns of the danger of offering sacrifices to demons and equates going after other gods with exposing oneself to demon activity by either ignorance of the consequences of "idols in the heart" (Ezek. 14:1–8) or through rebellion (1 Sam. 15:23).

Even as believers in Jesus Christ, it is possible we might foolishly be detoured or deceived by our flesh to offer subtle sacrifices to demons by making room for sin in our lives. Subtle moral and spiritual compromise can be the same thing as offering sacrifices to demons.

How can things like reading horoscopes, drinking alcohol, taking drugs, or watching violent or pornographic movies be the same as offering sacrifices to demons?

Whenever a believer in Jesus Christ begins to walk in darkness, in even the smallest area of his or her life, a doorway is opened into the spiritual realm for demonic control (Eph. 4:27). Small compromises can constitute sacrifices to demons because they are idolatrous in nature and involve deifying things (for example, self, sex, and pleasure) rather than Jesus Christ as Lord!

PERSONAL AND SEXUAL HOLINESS
(Leviticus 18:1—20:27)

The laws of sexual morality were outlined in Leviticus 18:1–30. Judeo-Christian morality, which upheld the exclusivity of sexual expression within the boundaries of a heterosexual marriage, has given way to a kind of new paganism. Now that we live in what some have termed a "post-Christian culture," the traditional sexual values adhered to by Judeo-Christian societies have given way to a sexual permissiveness that has opened the floodgates of sexual sin. Rape, sexual molestation of children, homosexuality, bestiality, incest, and abortion are all part of a massive cultural shift. In short, there is no longer any philosophical reason to deny any sexual urge, no matter how dark.

Read Leviticus 18:1–30 and list the verses that deal with the following issues and what God's opinion is regarding each.

1. Incest (verses)_____/ God's opinion_____

_____

2. Adultery (verses)_____ / God's opinion_____

_____

3. Homosexuality (verses)_____ / God's opinion_____

_____

In speaking of sexual perversion and idolatry, Leviticus 18:25 states, "For the land is defiled; therefore I visit the punishment of its iniquity upon it, and the land vomits out its inhabitants."

After reading the above verse, write briefly an explanation about what the term "vomits out its inhabitants" meant. Also, in your own words, describe how this could apply today in light of our society's emphasis on sexual perversion and idolatry.

Read Leviticus 19:1–37 and note how specific instructions to the people taught them to be holy as God is holy. Pay special attention to Leviticus 19:2 where God says, "Speak to all the congregation of the children of Israel, and say to them: "You shall be holy, for I the LORD your God *am* holy."

WORD WEALTH

Holy, *qadosh*. Set apart, dedicated to sacred purposes; holy, sacred, clean, morally or ceremonially pure. The verb *qadosh* means "to set apart something or someone for holy purposes." Holiness is separation from everything profane and defiling; and at the same time, it is dedication to everything holy and pure. People or even objects, such as anointing oil or vessels, may be considered holy to the Lord (Ex. 30:25; Jer. 2:3; Zech. 14:20, 21). Leviticus stresses "holy" and "holiness" most thoroughly. Lev. 10:10 shows that God desired that the priests be able to distinguish "holy" and "unholy" and teach Israel to do likewise. God is entirely holy in His nature, motives, thoughts, words, and deeds so that He is called *Qadosh*, "the Holy One," or *Qedosh Yisrael*, "the Holy One of Israel." Thus 19:2 can say, "You shall be *qedoshim* (holy ones) for I . . . am holy."[1]

After reading verse 19:2 and studying the above "Word Wealth," the following questions will help us to probe deeper into the truths regarding holiness:

How did practicing the various duties described help the people to imitate God's holiness?

In your own words, what does it mean when it says, "You shall be holy"?

Specifically, how did keeping these commandments keep the people holy?

In a very real sense, how does holiness produce both psychological and spiritual wholeness and well-being?

In our modern society, many people view being "religious" as keeping a list of "dos" and "don'ts." Is this what God had in mind when He called us to be holy? Explain the difference between mere list keeping and the walking in purity and power that real holiness produces.

Read Leviticus 19:26, 28, 31. Why were specific warnings given about occult involvement?

Leviticus 19:31 states, "Give no regard to mediums and familiar spirits; do not seek after them, to be defiled by them: I *am* the LORD." Why does God give this commandment, and how are people defiled by occult involvement?

Leviticus 19:29 says, "Do not prostitute your daughter, to cause her to be harlot, lest the land fall into harlotry, and the land become full of wickedness." That verse has powerful applications to our society today. How can certain things we allow our children to see and do cause them to be sexually impure and to "fall into harlotry"?

If, as parents, we allow our children to be raised by the entertainment industry, is that the same as "prostituting" one's daughter? See Leviticus 19:29.

Also, keeping verse 29 in mind, why is it crucial that we give our children positive and biblical information regarding sex?

Read Leviticus 19:35–37. How is social and legal justice a priority with God?

LAWS AND SACRIFICE FOR PRIESTS
(Leviticus 21:1—22:33)

After reading Leviticus 21:1—22:33, decide what is the central theme of these passages.

Leviticus 22:2 has a special warning for priests and leaders. What is that warning, and how does it apply to Christian leaders today who serve in any capacity before God's people?

How does the above verse give us a warning to preserve our individual holiness before the Lord?

 FAITH ALIVE

Leviticus 22:2 says, "Speak to Aaron and his sons, that they separate themselves from the holy things of the children of Israel, and they do not profane My holy name *by* what they dedicate to Me: I *am* the LORD." Then in verse 3 there is a warning about being cut off from the presence of God.

Spend a few moments in prayer before the Lord. Begin by praising Him and worshiping Him. Ask Him to fill you with His presence. Then ask Him to show you anything in your life that could cut you off from His presence. If He reveals any problem area to you by the light of His Holy Spirit, confess it before Him as sin. Do not deny it or attempt to justify it. Simply admit before God what He says about it and ask to be cleansed by the blood of Jesus Christ.

Finally, through the power of His Holy Spirit, ask Him to help you obey Him and do what He requests of you. Have confidence in the fact that God is working inside of you to help you to obey Him. Philippians 1:6 give us this promise: **"He who has begun a good work in you will complete** *it* **until the day of Jesus Christ."**

HOLY DAYS AND RELIGIOUS FEASTS
(Leviticus 23:1–44)

 AT A GLANCE

Feast	Month of Sacred Year	Day	Corresponding Month
ISRAEL'S ANNUAL FEASTS[2]			
Passover	1 (Abib)	14	Mar.–Apr.
Ex. 12:1–14; Lev. 23:5; Num. 9:1–14; 28:16 Deut. 16:1–7			
*Unleavened Bread	1 (Abib)	15–21	Mar.–Apr.
Ex. 12:15–20; 13:3–10; Lev. 23:6–8; Num. 28:17–25; Deut. 16:3, 4, 8			
Firstfruits	1 (Abib) and	16	Mar.–Apr.
	3 (Sivan)	6	May–June
Lev. 23:9–14; Num. 28:26			
*Weeks	3 (Sivan)	6 (50 days after	May–June
(Harvest or Pentecost)		barley harvest)	
Ex. 23:16; 34:22; Lev. 23:15–21; Num. 28:26–31; Deut. 16:9–12			
Trumpets	7 (Tishri)	1	Sept.–Oct.
Rosh Hashanah			
Lev. 23:23–25; Num. 29:1–6			
Day of Atonement	7 (Tishri)	10	Sept.–Oct.
Yom Kippur			
Lev. 16; 23:26–32; Num. 29:7–11			
*Tabernacles	7 (Tishri)	15–22	Sept.–Oct.
(Booths or Ingathering)			
Ex. 23:16; 34:22; Lev. 23:33–36, 39–43; Num. 29:12–38; Deut. 16:13–15			
*The three major feasts for which all males of Israel were required to travel to the temple in Jerusalem (Ex. 23:14–19).			

Leviticus 23:1 and 2 stated, "And the LORD spoke to Moses, saying, 'Speak to the children of Israel, and say to them: "The feasts of the LORD, which you shall proclaim *to be* holy convocations, these *are* my feasts." ' "

Read Leviticus 23. List the various feasts and what they taught:

1.

2.

3.

4.

5.

6.

7.

The annual feasts of Israel have significance for our generation today, as well as for the children of Israel. The apostle Paul said, "For whatever things were written before were written for our learning, that we through patience and comfort of the Scriptures might have hope" (Rom. 15:4).

Also, in Colossians 2:16 and 17, "So let no one judge you in food or drink, or regarding a festival or a new moon or sabbaths, which are a shadow of things to come, but the substance is of Christ." In light of the fact that the apostle Paul says that a "festival" and "sabbaths" are "a shadow of things to come," these feasts have both a historical and a prophetic role.

What was the prophetic role of the Feast of Passover? (1 Cor. 5:7)

How did the Feast of Unleavened Bread foreshadow the believer's deliverance from sin and bondage by Jesus Christ?

Read 1 Corinthians 15:20–23. How did the Feast of Firstfruits foreshadow what would happen at Christ's second coming?

How is the Feast of Pentecost prophetic of the church? (Acts 2:1–4)

On the Day of Atonement, or *Yom Kippur*, the high priest went into the Holy of Holies where he applied the blood of the sin offering to the mercy seat for the sins of the people (Lev. 16:14). How did this feast foreshadow the death and resurrection of Jesus Christ?

What happened to the "scapegoat"? (Lev. 16:21, 22)

LAWS FOR RELIGIOUS ELEMENTS AND PUNISHMENT FOR BLASPHEMY (Leviticus 24:1–23)

Leviticus 24:2 says, "Command the children of Israel that they bring to you pure oil of pressed olives for the light, to make the lamps burn continually." How does this scripture contrast with the Parable of the Wise and Foolish Virgins in Matthew 25:1–13?

Study Matthew 25:1–13. How does this parable present a picture of revival before the second coming of Jesus Christ?

Apply the truth of Matthew 25:1–13 and Leviticus 24:2 to your own life. What practical steps can you take to make sure that you have the "pure oil" of the Holy Spirit burning brightly in your life?

How can you be like the wise virgins who had oil in their lamps when the bridegroom returned? How does this truth apply to your life as you live in an age of spiritual darkness and moral blindness?

ISRAEL'S OTHER SACRED TIMES
(Leviticus 25:1–55)

The sacred times of Israel (see chart on p. 40 of Lesson 3) had both practical and commemorative purposes. In your own words, describe the economic, physical, and biological benefits of observing the following sacred times. What was the purpose of obeying the Sabbath?

What would have been the purpose agriculturally of the Sabbath Year?

Our modern economy deals with debt reduction through depression, recession, and inflation. How did obeying the Year of Jubilee positively affect Israel's economy?

REWARDS FOR OBEDIENCE AND
PUNISHMENT FOR DISOBEDIENCE
(Leviticus 26:1–46)

Study Leviticus 26:1–13 and read the promises of tremendous blessing upon God's people *if* they obeyed the covenant.

What was one of the primary conditions of their blessing? (Lev. 26:3)

What was God's promise regarding material blessing? (Lev. 26:3–5)

Leviticus 26:6 reads, "I will give you peace in the land, and you shall lie down, and none will make *you* afraid." Leviticus 26:36, 37 says, "And as for those of you who are left, I will send faintness into their hearts in the lands of their enemies; the sound of a shaken leaf shall cause them to flee; they shall flee as though fleeing from a sword, and they shall fall when no one pursues. They shall stumble over one another, as it were before a sword, when no one pursues; and you shall have no *power* to stand before your enemies."

The above Scripture verses describe two entirely different responses regarding fear. In your own words, write down the differences between the two responses and the reason for them.

Read Leviticus 26:14–39. What is the difference between the covenant relationship here and in Leviticus 26:1–13?

What is the key to receiving God's blessings, and how can we avoid the curses?

Having read Leviticus 26, it is important that we understand something about God's character. Is God just sitting up in heaven waiting to pour out blessings or "zap" people if they disobey? Since the Bible teaches that God is good, why do these curses come about if people disobey Him?

Is it ever God's will that His people suffer the negative things that disobedience brings?

How does this covenant concept relate to God's protective hand and covering upon His people versus His hand of protection being removed through disobedience? Is God "zapping" people with curses, or is His divine protection simply being removed so that people suffer the results of natural consequences and real attacks from Satan?

PROBING THE DEPTHS

In Acts 10:38 we read something of God's character toward people: "How God anointed Jesus of Nazareth with the Holy Spirit and with power, who went about doing good and healing all who were oppressed by the devil, for God was with Him." Here we see that it is the Devil who oppresses. God wants to save people. In John 10:10 this theme is repeated in Jesus' words, "The thief does not come except to steal, and to kill, and to destroy. I have come that they might have life, and that they might have *it* more abundantly."

Also in Genesis 3:1–15, we see how it was Satan who tempted man to disobey God, and the result was a curse on the human race. After reading Genesis 3, answer the following questions:

Since God created man for paradise and tremendous blessing, who released a curse on the human race?

Was it God's will for humankind to be under a curse?

How could Adam and Eve have avoided actuating a curse?

What was Satan's or the serpent's role in this?

GIFTS TO THE SANCTUARY
(Leviticus 27:1–34)

After reading Leviticus 27, write a brief answer to the question, "Why is it important for me to keep my vows and commitments to the Lord?"

AT A GLANCE

TRUTH-IN-ACTION through LEVITICUS[3]

Letting the LIFE of the Holy Spirit Bring Faith's Works Alive in You!

Truth Leviticus Teaches	Text	**Action** Leviticus Invites
1 Steps to Dynamic Devotion God wants our devotion for Him to guide the way we live. The Bible suggests many ways to build a life that expresses zealous devotion for God. A devoted life focuses on knowing and pleasing God.	3:1 6:12, 13	**Know** that fellowship with God requires time, energy, and resources we would normally use otherwise. **Be constant** in your zeal for the Lord and His kingdom. Half-hearted devotion is unworthy (see Rev. 3:16).
2 Keys to Effective Service Lev. is a book on service. It has much to say to the believer about how God wants all spiritual ministry to be conducted. Since every believer is called to be a ministering person (see Eph. 4:11–16), these guidelines are highly important.	1:3 2:1 19:19 19:23–25 24:1–4 25:46	**Serve** the Lord with the best of your efforts. **Make sure** that your ministry is without the defects of pride, selfish ambition, or a personal lack of holiness. **Soak** all ministry with continuous prayer (incense) and **be filled** with the Holy Spirit (oil) while engaged in any ministry activity. **Avoid** mixing Spirit-filled and fleshly activity in the conduct of your ministry. God abhors such a mixture. **Do not urge** the immature to enter ministry prematurely. Long-term fruitfulness may be limited. **Be ready** constantly to bear witness to your faith in Jesus as Lord and Savior. Leaders, **minister** with meekness, gentleness, and humility. Harsh, overbearing leadership misrepresents God's character and nature.
3 Keys to Moral Purity Moral impurity is extremely destructive to spiritual life and personal relationships. Sexual unfaithfulness is often an analogy for idolatry and unfaithfulness in the OT. Impurity compromises the integrity of our minds, hearts, and bodies. God tells us to flee from it because of its evil power.	11:47; 15:31 18:1–30	**Avoid** all spiritual and moral uncleanness. It will corrupt and defile every aspect of your life. **Know** what God's Word says about sexual conduct. **Flee** from and **avoid** every form of sexual and moral uncleanness.

	20:13	**Know** God's attitude about homosexuality. It is a serious perversion. Though He offers grace to the homosexual offender, He rejects his conduct.
4 **Guidelines for Godly Living** Though often concerned with the types of Hebrew ceremonial and ritual laws, Lev. can prove helpful for any believer who is serious about learning to live a life that is godly in Christ Jesus. Lev. makes it clear that godliness is not optional for those who want to live in a way that pleases their Lord.	4:2, 13, 22, 27	**Acknowledge** that you are inclined to sin by your very nature.
	7:6, 28–36	**Honor** God's servants with adequate financial support.
	19:32	**Honor** your parents. **Shun** the kind of disregard for elderly parents that the world promotes.
	26:1–46	**Study** and **know** God's Word. **Practice** it faithfully. God blesses obedience, but considers unfaithfulness <u>hostility</u> to Him.
	27:1–8	**Know** that God puts special value on everyone He has redeemed.
5 **Keys to Dealing with Sin** Like cancer, sin can spread quickly and defile a whole church or nation. God commands that we deal with sin forthrightly and thoroughly. Only through confronting sin can we ever be saved from its power. God cannot look upon sin because of His holiness, so we should not overlook it or deal with it lightly.	5:1; 19:17	**Do not conceal** wrongdoing you are aware of. **Confront** sin.
	5:2–4	**Know** that you are accountable even for sins you are not aware of. **Be sensitive** to the Holy Spirit's conviction of sin, and **repent** when convicted.
	5:5; 26:40	**Confess** your sins quickly, frankly, and openly. Hiding them will only harden your heart.
	6:5	Whenever possible, **make restitution** for sins you have committed against others, as a part of genuine repentance.

1. *Spirit-Filled Life Bible* (Nashville, TN: Thomas Nelson Publishers, 1991), 171, "Word Wealth: 19:2 holy."

2. Ibid., 178, Chart: "Israel's Annual Feasts."

3. Ibid., 186–187, "Truth-in-Action through Leviticus."

Lesson 8/Instructions for the Journey from Sinai (Num. 1:1—10:10)

The Fourth Book of Moses, called Numbers, was written about 1400 B.C. by Moses. Events in the book take place within a forty-year period, shortly after the Exodus in 1440 B.C. The Book of Numbers deals with Israel's journey from Sinai to Transjordan. According to the introduction of the Book of Numbers from the *Spirit-Filled Life Bible,* "One of the most familiar events in Numbers is the negative report of the ten spies, as opposed to the positive one of Joshua and Caleb (13:25–33). This resulted in severe chastisement (14:20–38). From this we learn the profound consequences that can sometimes develop from being faithless and negative. **When God speaks a promise, we need to respond with optimism, not pessimism.**

"The repeated grumblings of the Israelites, even in light of God's continuous provision, show us the need to maintain an attitude of thankfulness to God, even when we have great needs (Phil. 4:6)."[1]

As we read the Book of Numbers, it is important that we do not just read a historical account, but that we apply the great truths of faith in God's Word even in the midst of trial and difficulty to our own lives. In a very real sense, the Book of Numbers shares great truths about how Jesus Christ is at work in our lives, taking us out of the wilderness and leading us through the Holy Spirit and the Word of God to the Promised Land. Therefore, as we read Numbers we must constantly ask ourselves the question, How do these truths apply to my life in the circumstances I now face as well as to the life of my family, friends, and nation?

THE TAKING OF THE MILITARY CENSUS
(Numbers 1:1—4:49)

The census deals with the formation of an army to invade the Promised Land. Numbers 1:18 was a public proclamation before all Israel to let people know who the people of God were. How does this public proclamation relate to Acts 18:8 where the people were publicly baptized?

Why is it important to make a public statement about your identification with God and the people of God?

Numbers 1:45 says that all the men were numbered who were able to go to war. The purpose of the census was not to get a count of large numbers so that the children of Israel could rely on human strength. It was to ask the question, "Who are the people of God?" First Samuel 14:6 states, "Then Jonathan said to the young man who bore his armor, 'Come, let us go over to the garrison of these uncircumcised; it may be that the LORD will work for us. For nothing restrains the LORD from saving by many or by few.'"

In your own words, write down the relationship between Numbers 1:45 and 1 Samuel 14:6.

What principle is God trying to teach us?

The children of Israel were placed by tribes around the tabernacle of meeting (Num. 2:2). Author and Bible teacher Chuck Missler comments that the camp of Israel, with the tabernacle in the middle, seems to be a model of the throne of God. In addition, Missler writes, "Judah's tribal standard was of course, the lion. Reuben's ensign was a man: Ephraim's was the ox. Dan's was ultimately, the eagle. . . . It is interesting to note that these four primary tribal standards—the lion, the man, the ox and the eagle—are the same as four faces of the cherubim."[2] Revelation 4:7 reads, "The first living creature *was* like a lion, the second living creature like a calf, the third living creature had a face like a man, and the fourth living creature *was* like a flying eagle." The interesting thing to note is that the Old Testament is filled with prophetic references to the New Testament. Obviously, this testifies to the supernatural authorship of the Bible, written by God through men who were divinely inspired by the Holy Spirit.

Also, an aerial view of the placement of the camps of Israel around the tabernacle of meeting shows that they make a perfect cross!

AT A GLANCE

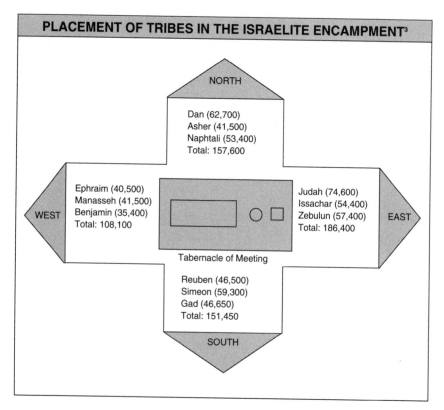

PLACEMENT OF TRIBES IN THE ISRAELITE ENCAMPMENT[3]

NORTH

Dan (62,700)
Asher (41,500)
Naphtali (53,400)
Total: 157,600

WEST

Ephraim (40,500)
Manasseh (41,500)
Benjamin (35,400)
Total: 108,100

Judah (74,600)
Issachar (54,400)
Zebulun (57,400)
Total: 186,400

EAST

Tabernacle of Meeting

Reuben (46,500)
Simeon (59,300)
Gad (46,650)
Total: 151,450

SOUTH

At the heart of Israel's being prepared militarily to invade the Promised Land was the tabernacle (Num. 3:5–8). Unlike other earthly armies, the army of Israel had the Lord as their source of strength, guidance, and wisdom. First Samuel 17:47 also reveals this spiritual principle that "the battle is the LORD's." Today, as believers in Jesus Christ, our battle is primarily spiritual. Just as with the tribes of Israel, God is our source of strength, wisdom, and guidance.

 FAITH ALIVE

Study 2 Corinthians 10:3, 4, which says, "For though we walk in the flesh, we do not war according to the flesh. For the weapons of our warfare *are* not carnal but mighty in God for the pulling down of strongholds."

How was the tabernacle of God, which was an earthly model of the throne room of God, the center of Israel's military operation?

What lesson should this teach us as New Testament believers who must engage in spiritual warfare? How is the throne room of God, which we can enter through the blood of Jesus Christ, the center of all of our wisdom and strength?

God's covenant required the offering of the firstborn. How does the taking of the Levites (Num. 3:12, 13) instead of the firstborn of the children of Israel satisfy this covenant?

How does Romans 8:29 relate to Numbers 3:12, 13?

How is the death and resurrection of Jesus Christ a fulfillment of this covenant?

SINLESSNESS AND BLESSING—THE CLOUD AND THE FIRE (Numbers 5:1—10:10)

Read Numbers 5:6, 7. What was a man or woman supposed to do if they sinned against the Lord?

How has Jesus Christ made a provision for us if we sin as the Holy Spirit leads us into a Promised Land? (1 John 1:9)

Numbers 5:11–31 speaks about the sexual unfaithfulness of wives. However, the Bible speaks about any kind of sexual sin, including the unfaithfulness of husbands, as being wrong. The Ten Commandments tell us, "You shall not commit adultery." Look up Malachi 2:13–16. How can unfaithfulness in marriage keep a person from receiving all that God has for them?

Malachi 2:13–16 states that God will not hear the prayers of a man who breaks covenant with his wife. After reading this passage, write in your own words how blessings and prayers can be blocked by disobedience in this area.

Numbers 6:22–27 describes the priestly blessing when it says, "And the LORD spoke to Moses, saying: 'Speak to Aaron and his sons, saying, "This is the way you shall bless the children of Israel. Say to them: 'The LORD bless you and keep you; the LORD make His face shine upon you, and be gracious to you; the LORD lift up His countenance upon you, and give you peace.'"' So they shall put My name on the children of Israel, and I will bless them."

After reading these passages of Scripture, describe in your own words why the power of blessing is not just a religious phrase.

Like Aaron, we have been given the power and authority to bless people in the name of Jesus Christ. How do we extend God's goodness and His kingdom rule in people's lives when we bless them?

How is the power of the Adversary crushed and God's power released when we speak blessing to people?

Why is it our responsibility to actively speak blessing into people's lives?

Read Numbers 8:1–4. In the earthly tabernacle, Aaron arranged seven lamps in front of the lampstand. How does this compare with Revelation 1:9–13, where we read about the seven gold lampstands, which represent the seven churches of the Apocalypse, placed before Jesus Christ?

How is the earthly tabernacle a model of the real, heavenly tabernacle that exists in heaven? (Heb. 9:1–5)

Numbers 9:15–19 describes how one of the promises of the covenant would be that the very presence of God would guide the children of Israel in a cloud by day and a fire by night. Both the cloud and the fire were manifestations of God's glory. How does this supernatural guidance compare with the inner witness of the Holy Spirit working in our lives?

How is the peace of God in our hearts a form of supernatural guidance in our lives today? (Phil. 4:7)

   FAITH ALIVE

Describe a time in your life when you experienced God's presence and glory speaking to you in a profound and powerful way. Take a few moments to recount that experience and write it down in your own words.

What was one of the main characteristics of that experience? How did it strengthen your faith?

Finally, spend a few minutes worshiping the Lord and thanking Him for His goodness in your life. With hands outstretched, begin to praise Him out loud for His goodness. Draw near to Him in worship and praise. Allow a fresh sense of His presence to permeate your being. Allow the glory of God to fill your life and to illuminate your paths.

Read Numbers 10:1–10. In verses 9 and 10 we see that the blowing of trumpets precedes victory. Verse 9 reads, "When you go to war in your land against the enemy who oppresses you, then you shall sound an alarm with the trumpets, and you will be remembered before the LORD your God, and you will be saved from your enemies." "The employment of trumpets has a unique relationship to the exercise of spiritual authority in prayer. Here two silver trumpets were sanctified for use by spiritual leadership in Israel. One was appointed for the calling forth of the assembly and the other for the mobilization of the camps when they were about to journey (v. 2). Thus, the first trumpet's use was primarily to gather the people together, while the second trumpet meant it was time to 'move forward,' usually in the sense of moving forward into battle."[4]

In our time, Christian leaders do not use trumpets to signal the people. However, after reflecting on the above truth, have there been occasions in your own life when you have heard the "trumpet call" of God in your life either through a leader or a circumstance? Take a moment and write down one or two examples of such times.

1. *Spirit-Filled Life Bible* (Nashville, TN: Thomas Nelson Publishers, 1991), 189, Introduction to Numbers.
2. Chuck Missler, *Personal Update* (the Newsletter of Koinonia House), February 1993, 11.
3. *Spirit-Filled Life Bible*, 193, Chart: "Placement of Tribes in the Israelite Encampment."
4. Ibid., 207, "Kingdom Dynamics: Trumpets and Spiritual Warfare."

Lesson 9/The Journey from Sinai (Num. 10:11—36:13)

AN UNBELIEVING GENERATION AND THE SLAVE MENTALITY (Numbers 10:11—25:18)

Numbers 10:11–36 tells of the account of the first march from Sinai. Verse 12 reads, "And the children of Israel set out from the Wilderness of Sinai on their journeys; then the cloud settled down in the Wilderness of Paran." After reading the above verse, write down in your own words what the purpose of the cloud of glory was as the children of Israel marched from Sinai.

Numbers 11:1 states, "Now *when* the people complained, it displeased the LORD; for the LORD heard *it,* and His anger was aroused. So the fire of the LORD burned among them, and consumed *some* in the outskirts of the camp." What powerful spiritual principle is revealed in the above verse?

In his Bible study series *Learning How to Live Again,* Dr. Jack Hayford goes into great detail about what he terms the *slave mentality.* One of the characteristics of this slave mentality is complaining. Slaves complain and grumble about things rather than believe God for the impossible and for victory. This truth is perhaps one of the greatest truths in the entire Bible. The key to miracles and unlocking God's power always lies along the path of belief in God's Word and walking in praise and worship. The fastest way out of any wilderness experience is to praise God in the midst of adversity and believe Him to move powerfully on your behalf.

Look up Jeremiah 33:3. What does the prophet Jeremiah tell us we are to do instead of complain?

What can we expect if we do what Jeremiah tells us to do?

Read Numbers 11:4–9, particularly verses 5 and 6. Why were the children of Israel complaining about not having enough "spice in their life"?

 FAITH ALIVE

How does this principle of complaining about "spice in life" parallel the believer's journey out of darkness into the kingdom of light?

As a believer in Jesus Christ, have you ever been tempted to look back to Egypt and long for the so-called "spice in life"? Perhaps you have been tempted to toy with sin in your mind or maybe to indulge a little here and there with things that are either outright sinful or just not very spiritually productive. Take a moment and write down areas where you may have had the slave mentality and longed for the spices of Egypt rather than the kingdom of God.

The key question is, How can we stay excited about the things of God and avoid the mistake that Israel made in the wilderness?

Finally, briefly describe how the cycle of grumbling and complaining leads to looking back to Egypt for the "spice in life," thus ending up with unbelief and sin in your life.

MOSES AS INTERCESSOR
(Numbers 12:1–16)

In Numbers 12:5–8, how does God establish Moses as His prophet with whom He will speak face to face and in dreams and visions?

What happens when Miriam and Aaron speak against Moses' spiritual leadership?

Verse 13 states, "So Moses cried out to the LORD, saying, 'Please heal her, O God, I pray!'" What does this verse show us about the power of being an intercessor and how our prayers can restore people who have sinned before God?

What is the warning to us about rebelling or speaking against legitimate spiritual leadership?

UNBELIEF AND FEAR BLOCK ENTRANCE TO THE PROMISED LAND
(Numbers 13:1—14:45)

Numbers 13:1, 2 records how spies were sent out into the Promised Land.

Numbers 13:27–29 records the evil or unbelieving report that the spies gave about conquering the Promised Land. "Then they told him, and said: 'We went to the land where you sent us. It truly flows with milk and honey, and this *is* its fruit. Nevertheless the people who dwell in the land *are* strong; the cities *are* fortified *and* very large; moreover we saw the descendants of Anak there. The Amalekites dwell in the land of the South; the Hittites, the Jebusites, and the Amorites dwell in the mountains; and the Canaanites dwell by the sea and along the banks of the Jordan.'"

After reading the above passages of Scripture, spend a moment and analyze what the spies said. What was the purpose of discussing in detail the strength of the enemy?

How did this report actually magnify the power of their enemy in their eyes?

How was this an evil report of unbelief? After all, weren't they simply giving the facts?

Contrast this evil report with the report of faith and belief that Caleb gave in verse 30 where it says, "Then Caleb quieted the people before Moses, and said, 'Let us go up at once and take possession, for we are well able to overcome it.'" What was the difference between Caleb's report of faith and the unbelieving report?

What actions did the two different reports produce?

How can we apply this truth in our lives personally? If God has given us a Promised Land, dream, or a vision, how can we make sure that we respond as Caleb did when he said,

"Let us go up at once and take possession, for we are well able to overcome it"?

Study Numbers 13:31–33. "But the men who had gone up with him said, 'We are not able to go up against the people, for they *are* stronger than we.' And they gave the children of Israel a bad report of the land which they had spied out, saying, 'The land through which we have gone as spies *is* a land that devours its inhabitants, and all the people whom we saw in it *are* men of *great* stature. There we saw giants (the descendants of Anak came from the giants); and we were like grasshoppers in our own sight, and so we were in their sight.'"

These passages diagram for us what an evil or unbelieving report is. Notice verse 33 where it says, "we were like grasshoppers in our own sight, and so we were in their sight." How did their nonbiblical and unbelieving perception of themselves reduce their power in the sight of their enemies?

It is vitally important that we understand that these passages of scripture were not just written for our historical understanding. The Holy Spirit has something to say to you and me when we read these scriptures. Write down the "Promised Land" or vision God has given you for your life. Then make sure you are perceiving this God-given goal with a renewed mind and a faith-filled or believing report.

 BIBLE EXTRA

Look up 1 Samuel 17:1–51. Notice the difference between David's response to the giant in the land and that of the unbelieving children of Israel. Instead of giving an evil or unbelieving report, David confidently said in verses 45 and 46, "Then David said to the Philistine, 'You come to me with a sword, with a spear, and with a javelin. But I come to you in the name of the LORD of hosts, the God of the armies of Israel, whom you have defied. This day the LORD will deliver you into my hand, and I will strike you and take your head from you. And this day I will give the carcasses of the camp of the Philistines to the birds of the air and the wild beasts of the earth, that all the earth may know that there is a God in Israel.'"

What was the difference between David's declaration of faith in the face of a giant and that of the children of Israel in Numbers 13:33?

What was the secret of David's boldness and faith? (1 Sam. 16:13)

How can we make sure as believers in Jesus Christ that we have an anointing of the Spirit of God, which produces faith and boldness?

Numbers 14:1–4 reveals that the children of Israel still had the slave mentality. How does verse 2 reveal the extent to which their minds and spirits were still in bondage to Egypt because they refused to believe God?

Numbers 14:6–9 tells how Joshua and Caleb gave a report of faith and obedience to God. Verse 8 states, "If the LORD delights in us, then He will bring us into this land and give it to us, a land which flows with milk and honey." Contrast this verse with Psalm 37:4 where it says to "Delight yourself also in the LORD." Write down in your own words the relationship between these truths.

Numbers 14:9 states, "Only do not rebel against the LORD, nor fear the people of the land, for they *are* our bread; their protection has departed from them, and the LORD *is* with us. Do not fear them." How can we apply that verse to our own lives? Write down three ways you can apply that verse to the circumstances you face.

1.

2.

3.

Read Numbers 14:11–20. What was the Lord saying to Moses about unbelief? (v. 11)

Look up Matthew 13:58. Compare what happened to Jesus Christ with Numbers 14:11 where the Lord says, "How long will these people reject Me?"

How does unbelief in our lives cause us to "reject" God?

In the earthly ministry of Jesus, what was the result of the people's unbelief? (Matt. 13:58)

Read Hebrews 3:12 and 19. After you have seen God's power at work, why is unbelief so dangerous?

What is Moses' response to the people's unbelief? (Num. 14:19)

What does this teach us about the role of an intercessor?

Numbers 14:18 says, "The LORD is longsuffering and abundant in mercy, forgiving iniquity and transgression; but He by no means clears *the guilty,* visiting the iniquity of the fathers on the children to the third and fourth *generation.*" Clearly, this verse reveals that the consequences of sin can be passed on from generation to generation. How can God's forgiveness of sin prevent this destruction from being passed on from one generation to another, and what is the role of an intercessor in this?

In my book *The Breakthrough Manual—How the power of miracles can break the generational curse, heal you from a dysfunctional past and totally set you free,* I seek to teach readers how to deal with the adverse effects of sin passed on from one generation to another. "It is impossible to understand or correct any problem in life without first understanding the ultimate origin of the problem. Fundamentally, we must understand that all of life's problems have a primary source. There is an actual death force which the Bible calls sin. Although modern man has dismissed the word sin as an archaic and medieval concept, it is a very real cosmic force responsible for the destruction of both people and society."[1] The good news is that the cycle of destruction that sin brings (discussed in Num. 14:18) can be removed by the blood of Jesus Christ. In other words, because of the death and resurrection of Christ upon the Cross, we no longer have to be slaves to sin's power.

Numbers 14:22–24 records the fact that God is not going to allow those who have seen His powerful signs and have chosen not to believe Him to enter the Promised Land. However, in verse 24 we read, "But My servant Caleb, because he has a different spirit in him and has followed Me fully, I will bring into the land where he went, and his descendants shall inherit it." How can we make sure that we have a "different spirit"—one other than the spirit of unbelief—in us? How can we make sure that we follow God "fully"?

Numbers 14:26–38 tells us that God is going to let an entire generation die off except for Caleb and Joshua before they enter the Promised Land. Why couldn't God bring this unbelieving generation into the Promised Land?

Verses 36 and 37 tell us that the men who made the congregation complain against Moses by bringing a bad report died by a plague. Why was the punishment so severe?

Numbers 14:39–45 gives a powerful warning against presumption. In verse 42 Moses warns the people, "Do not go up, lest you be defeated by your enemies, for the LORD is not among you." The response of the people can be found in verse 44 where it says, "But they presumed to go up to the mountaintop." What does this passage of Scripture teach us about the danger of doing what appears to be right rather than what God has specifically commanded us to do?

What were the consequences of the presumption of the children of Israel?

What is the difference between presumption and faith?

INSTRUCTIONS CONCERNING OFFERINGS
(Numbers 15:1–41)

Numbers 15:25 states, "So the priest shall make atonement for the whole congregation of the children of Israel, and it shall be forgiven them, for it was unintentional; they shall bring their offering, an offering made by fire to the LORD, and their sin offering before the LORD, for their unintended sin."

 WORD WEALTH

Make atonement, *chaphar.* To cover, make atonement, make reconciliation; to pacify or appease; to clear, purge, or cleanse. This verb occurs 100 times. The primary meaning of *chaphar* may be to "cover." The verb is used in Genesis 6:14, where Noah was instructed to cover the ark with pitch. An important derivative is the word *kippur* (atonement), a familiar term due to its use in *Yom Kippur,* the Day of Atonement.[2]

Yom Kippur is the Day of Atonement. How did Jesus Christ make "atonement" for our sins?

GOD CONFIRMS SPIRITUAL AUTHORITY
(Numbers 16:1—18:32)

In Numbers 16:3 some of the children of Israel rebelled against the God-given authority of Moses and Aaron. "They gathered together against Moses and Aaron, and said to them, *You take* too much upon yourselves, for all the congregation *is* holy, every one of them, and the LORD *is* among them. Why then do you exalt yourselves above the assembly of the LORD?"

BIBLE EXTRA

Clearly, the Bible does not teach blind obedience to spiritual leaders. There have been abuses of spiritual authority. Yet the Bible teaches that God does call men to positions of leadership and spiritual authority.

Explain how Numbers 16:3 illustrates rebellion against legitimate spiritual authority?

What was God's reaction to the rebellion against His divine chain of command? (vv. 20, 21)

How does verse 22 reveal the role of an intercessor?

Read Numbers 16:28–33. Why did God cause the earth to swallow up those who were in rebellion?

Read Acts 5:1–11 which records the story of Ananias and Sapphira who lied to God and fell dead. There are times in the Bible when people rebel against God and His authority. Then judgment comes. God is longsuffering, and Jesus Christ forgives sins. However, what does the Bible say about continual rebellion from God?

Read Numbers 17:1–13. In verses 7 and 8 we read, "And Moses placed rods before the LORD in the tabernacle of witness. Now it came to pass on the next day that Moses went into the tabernacle of witness, and behold, the rod of Aaron, of the house of Levi, had sprouted and put forth buds, had produced blossoms and yielded ripe almonds." How did the budding of Aaron's rod show how God can back up spiritual leadership with signs and wonders?

What is the similarity between Numbers 17:7, 8 and 2 Corinthians 12:12, which says, "Truly the signs of an apostle were accomplished among you with all perseverance, in signs and wonders and mighty deeds"?

Numbers 18:21 states, "Behold, I have given the children of Levi all the tithes of Israel as an inheritance in return for the work which they perform, the work of the tabernacle of meeting." How does this verse teach that those who are in the ministry are entitled to be supported by the tithes of the people?

Compare and contrast this with the provisions of the New Testament. (1 Cor. 9:1–14)

Laws of Purification
(Numbers 19:1–22)

The laws of purification concerned instructions for purification of people who touch corpses. This chapter relates to Numbers 16 where the people who rebelled died. However, this chapter illustrates that God is not on the side of death. Obviously, believers in Jesus Christ would not need to slaughter a heifer as in verses 2 and 3. Yet believers in Jesus Christ must regularly confess their sins before their High Priest Jesus Christ so that they will not be infected with spiritual death.

Look up 1 John 1:7 in the New Testament and Numbers 19:1–5 in the Old Testament. How is the blood that is spilled for the sins of the people in Numbers 19:1–5 a foreshadowing of the truth in 1 John 1:7?

After studying the above verses, why is it important to confess our sins to the Lord quickly? What is the result if we do not?

Moses at Kadesh: The Danger of Acting on Past
Experience Rather Than Fresh Revelation
(Numbers 20:7–13)

In Numbers 20:7–13 Moses took the rod, struck the rock, and water came out abundantly. Although God used Moses to perform this miracle, God was not pleased with Moses for disobeying and not believing in God's ability to "hallow Himself in the eyes of the children of Israel." After reading this verse of Scripture, write down briefly an explanation of how Moses, who was acting on the basis of his past experience, missed out on the new thing that God was doing.

What did this mistake cost Moses? (v. 12)

What is the lesson we must learn about not resting on past experiences of revival, revelation, and blessing?

How can we make sure that we continually move with God in fresh anointing?

THE BRONZE SERPENT
(Numbers 21:1–35)

In Numbers 21:4–9 the children of Israel again complained and spoke against God and Moses. As a result, God sent fiery serpents against them and they were bitten and became sick. Verse 6 states, "So the LORD sent fiery serpents among the people, and they bit the people; and many of the people of Israel died." What did these fiery serpents represent?

AT A GLANCE

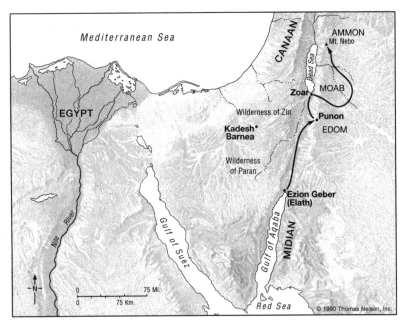

From the Wilderness to Canaan[3]

How can we walk out from under God's protective covering in our own lives and become prey to demonic forces by disobeying God's Word?

Verse 7 shows that Moses interceded for the people. As a result, verse 8 says, "Then the LORD said to Moses, 'Make a fiery *serpent,* and set it on a pole; and it shall be that everyone who is bitten, when he looks at it, shall live.'" How does this verse relate to John 3:14, 15 and 1 Peter 2:24 where it says, "By whose stripes you were healed"?

How does the pole represent the cross of Christ and the serpent on it signify that Jesus Christ destroyed the powers of darkness on the cross?

Modern medicine uses as its symbol the pole with a serpent. How does the healing power of Jesus Christ on the cross relate to this symbol?

BALAK AND BALAAM
(Numbers 22:1—25:18)

Read Numbers 22:22–35. In this account of Balaam, the Angel, and the donkey, we learn that Balaam's way was blocked by the Angel of the Lord. In verse 23 we read, "Now the donkey saw the Angel of the LORD standing in the way with His drawn sword in His hand, and the donkey turned aside out of the way and went into the field. So Balaam struck the donkey to turn her back onto the road."

Here we learn that it was God who supernaturally blocked Balaam's path. What was Balaam's response to his donkey's turning aside?

Verse 27 again reveals Balaam's response to the donkey. As a prophet of God who was seeking to be led by God, what should have been Balaam's response to the donkey?

Could Balaam have recognized that his problem with the donkey was a divine delay rather than a merely natural one?

In verse 31 we read, "Then the LORD opened Balaam's eyes, and he saw the Angel of the LORD standing in the way with His drawn sword in His hand; and he bowed his head and fell flat on his face." As a prophet of God, shouldn't Balaam and not his donkey have been the one to see the Angel of the Lord?

In your own words, write down a brief explanation of what God was trying to teach Balaam through this incident. Pay special attention to verses 32 and 34.

Read Numbers 24:1–9. In Numbers 24 the Spirit of God came upon Balaam, and he prophesied correctly. Although Balak had hired Balaam to curse Israel, Balaam could not do it. Why couldn't Balaam curse Israel? (Num. 23:8, 20, 23)

 FAITH ALIVE

Many times in our Christian walk we ask God for His plan for our lives. In addition, we ask God to lead us and open doors for us if it is His will for our lives. However, there are times like that in the life of Balaam when God supernaturally closes a door or divinely blocks our path.

Recount the times in your life when you have asked God to lead you and you have experienced either open doors or shut doors. Using the list below, write down three open doors that you knew God had opened for you and write down three doors that you believe God shut. Then in the right-hand column, write down the reason you believe God either opened or shut those doors in your life.

DOORS GOD OPENED IN YOUR LIFE	THE REASON WHY
1. Example: God opened the door financially for you to go to school.	To prepare you to be a teacher so that you could help shape and mold young lives.
2.	
3.	

DOORS GOD SHUT IN YOUR LIFE	THE REASON WHY
1. God supernaturally blocked your path in a business career.	You were called to the ministry and were not sensitive to His call so He got your attention through closed doors.
2.	
3.	

1. From *The Breakthrough Manual—How the power of miracles can break the generational curse, heal you from a dysfunctional past and totally set you free,* copyright 1993 by Paul McGuire (South Plainfield, NJ: Bridge Publishing), 4. Used with Permission.

2. *Spirit-Filled Life Bible* (Nashville, TN: Thomas Nelson Publishers, 1991), 217, "Word Wealth: 15:25 make atonement."

3. Ibid., map on 225.

Lesson 10/The New Generation
(Num. 26:1—36:13)

A New Census
(Numbers 26:1–65)

A new census was taken because the first generation had perished in the wilderness. A new generation is prepared for entrance into the Promised Land. After reading Numbers 26:1–65, go back and look up Numbers 14:30. Answer the question, Why did an entire generation have to die off in the the wilderness before this new generation could enter the Promised Land?

In Numbers 13 and 14, we are given a number of reasons why an entire generation of Israel was not allowed to enter the Promised Land. Listed below are some Scripture verses from these chapters that reveal why they could not enter. In your own words, write down next to the verse a short explanation of why these actions or words were spiritually harmful.

Verse: **Explanation:**

Num. 13:28

Num. 13:31

Num. 13:33

Num. 14:2

In this new generation that is going into the Promised Land, no more murmurings, complaints, or rebellions are recorded.

JOSHUA, THE LEADER OF A NEW GENERATION
(Numbers 27:1—30:16)

In Numbers 27 Joshua becomes the leader of a new generation. Carefully study this chapter about how God selects and ordains a leader. It is important to understand that Joshua was chosen for leadership, not out of any human selection, but he was divinely appointed by God.

Verse 16 says, "Let the LORD, the God of the spirits of all flesh, set a man over the congregation." Notice that it is God who is doing the setting. What does this verse tell us about how a man should be set in leadership over any church?

In verse 18 we read, "And the LORD said to Moses: 'Take Joshua the son of Nun with you, a man in whom *is* the Spirit, and lay your hand on him.'" Notice the key words "a man in whom *is* the Spirit." Clearly, in addition to God's choice of Joshua, the Spirit of God was in him. What does this passage of Scripture tell us about another prerequisite for leadership?

Verse 23 states, "And he laid his hands on him and inaugurated him, just as the LORD commanded by the hand of Moses." Read 1 Timothy 4:14. In your own words, write down a brief statement of why, in both the Old and New Testaments, the laying on of hands was an essential part of establishing leadership.

VENGEANCE ON THE MIDIANITES
(Numbers 31:1–54)

In Numbers 31:2 God spoke to Moses, saying, "Take vengeance on the Midianites for the children of Israel. . . ." Read chapter 31 and then go back to Numbers 25:1–18. In light of Numbers 25, give an explanation in your own words of why Moses required the children of Israel to kill the Midianite men and women.

What would have happened to Israel if they had continued to "commit harlotry with the women of Moab" (Num. 25:1) and sacrifice to their gods? (Num. 25:2)

THE TRIBES SETTLING EAST OF JORDAN
(Numbers 32:1–42)

In Numbers 32:7–23 Moses gives the children of Israel a refresher course in faith and believing God. Briefly explain why discouraging the heart of God's people is a serious sin. (v. 7)

FAITH ALIVE

Now apply that truth to your own life and answer the question, Have you or anybody you have known ever discouraged other believers through the careless use of your tongue?

Read James 3:1–12. Write down how you can keep from discouraging God's people through your words.

Read Numbers 32:11–23. What lesson was Moses trying to teach the children of Israel which they should have already learned?

What steps could the children of Israel take in order not to sin before the Lord? (vv. 20–23)

ISRAEL'S JOURNEY FROM EGYPT REVIEWED
(Numbers 33:1–49)

How did the children of Israel go out in the sight of all the Egyptians? (v. 3)

On whom did the Lord execute judgment? (v. 4)

OPERATION CANAAN
(Numbers 33:50—36:13)

God gives the Israelites instructions for the conquest of Canaan. He is the covenant-keeping God. He will drive out their enemies before them if they have faith in His promises. God gives promises to believers today. If we are faithful to God, He will drive out our enemies before us and give us the Promised Land.

Numbers 33:50–53 records the specific instructions God gave to Moses to speak to the children of Israel. What were they to do to the idols? (v. 52) Why?

PROBING THE DEPTHS

Numbers 35:33, 34 states, "So you shall not pollute the land where you *are;* for blood defiles the land, and no atonement can be made for the land, for the blood that is shed on it, except by the blood of him who shed it. Therefore do not defile the land which you inhabit, in the midst of which I dwell; for I the LORD dwell among the children of Israel."

Several profound truths are revealed in these verses. Go back to Genesis 4:8–10 to the story of Cain and Abel. Cain murdered his brother Abel. Genesis 4:10 says, "And He said, 'What have you done? The voice of your brother's blood cries out to Me from the ground.'" This verse of Scripture directly relates to Numbers 35:33 where it says "blood defiles the land." Clearly, God is talking about a casual relationship between the earth and murder. In other words, God's presence actually dwells upon the earth to bless it as He did in the Garden of Eden. However, sin—especially a hideous sin such as murder—actually drives away the presence of God from the earth. Therefore, the land is cursed or defiled.

Genesis 4:11, 12 states, "So now you *are* cursed from the earth, which has opened its mouth to receive your brother's blood from your hand. When you till the ground, it shall no longer yield its strength to you. . . ." This relationship between the productivity of the earth and God's covenant blessing is further explained in Deuteronomy 28. It is always God's will to bless His people abundantly. However, sin violates the covenant, and God's blessings are removed unless atonement is made.

FAITH ALIVE

First Corinthians 10:11 states, "Now all these things happened to them as examples, and they were written for our admonition, upon whom the ends of the ages have come." Just as it was God's will for the children of Israel to enter the Promised Land, so it is His will that believers in Jesus Christ enter the Promised Land of purpose and destiny that He has intended for them.

However, Numbers teaches us that disobedience and sin can keep us from inheriting the promises of God.

Lesson 11/Moses' First Message
(Deut. 1:1—4:43)

According to tradition, Deuteronomy, or the Fifth Book of Moses, was written by Moses approximately 1400 B.C. The last chapter, which is an account of Moses' death, was probably written by Joshua. Deuteronomy consists of a series of farewell addresses by Moses as he attempts to prepare the children of Israel for entrance into the Promised Land. Moses tells the people thirty-five times to "go in and possess the land." Moses reminds them of the covenant relationship that God had made with them starting with Abraham, Isaac, and Jacob.

In Deuteronomy, Moses fervently exhorts the people to obey the conditions of the covenant so that they will prosper. They are warned against idolatry and disobedience. Prior to entering into the Promised Land, the children of Israel know full well that if they worship God as Lord and obey Him, then they will prosper and be in health. Conversely, if they disobey Him, then they will experience adversity, death, poverty, sickness, and destruction. The rules that God places before them are quite simple. The Israelites know precisely what God was requiring of them.

Before his death, Moses implores the people many times to remember that obedience will bring blessing, and disobedience will bring a curse. They are reminded that God is a covenant-keeping God. If they will keep God's covenant everything will go well with them.

THE LAND SET BEFORE THEM
(Deuteronomy 1:1—2:25)

In Deuteronomy 1:8 we read, "See, I have set the land before you; go in and possess the land which the LORD swore to your fathers—to Abraham, Isaac, and Jacob—to give them and their descendants after them." How does this passage of Scripture reveal that the Promised Land is a fulfillment of God's covenant established centuries before?

God is a covenant-keeping God, and in His Word He promised to give the Israelites the land. Likewise, God gives us promises through His Word. What is our responsibility in relationship to God's Word?

Read Deuteronomy 1:13. How does this passage of Scripture reveal the principle of delegating authority?

Write down three of the requirements for choosing spiritual leaders. (v. 13)

1.

2.

3.

How does this compare with the New Testament principle of appointing spiritual leaders? (1 Cor. 12:28)

Take a few minutes to study Deuteronomy 1:13 and 1 Corinthians 12:28. After reading both of these passages of Scripture, write down in your own words how God delegates spiritual authority to men.

What should our response be to legitimate spiritual authority?

 BEHIND THE SCENES

In addition to these gifts, God has also appointed elders for the local church. Titus 1:5 says, "For this reason I left you in Crete, that you should set in order the things that are lacking, and appoint elders in every city as I commanded you." Clearly, delegation and spiritual authority are God-ordained principles. Even in the invisible realm God has established a chain of command. Daniel 10:13 states, "But the prince of the kingdom of Persia withstood me twenty-one days; and behold, Michael, one of the chief princes, came to help me, for I had been left alone there with the kings of Persia." Here and in Revelation 12:7, where it says, "Michael and his angels fought," we find that God has a special chain of command among His angels. What this tells us is that God has a divine government with a delegated authority. Here on earth God has given certain men delegated authority. However, the difference between God's government and Satanic, or mere earthly governments, is that God's rule is always characterized by love and servanthood, never "lording it over" someone.

Jesus Christ was our ultimate example of this when He laid down His life for us. Even in the marriage relationship there is delegated authority. However, once again the authority is based on servanthood with Christ as the example. Ephesians 5:25 states, "Husbands, love your wives, just as Christ also loved the church and gave Himself for her."

Once again the lesson of faith in God's covenant promise of deliverance is recounted. This lesson will be taught over and over again because of its absolute priority in the life of God's people—then, as well as today. Deuteronomy 1:28–30 says, "Where can we go up? Our brethren have discouraged our hearts, saying, 'The people *are* greater and taller than we; the cities *are* great and fortified up to heaven; moreover we have seen the sons of Anakim there.' Then I said to you, 'Do not be terrified, or afraid of them. The LORD your God, who goes before you, He will fight for you, according to all He did for you in Egypt before your eyes.'"

Study this passage on faith vs. fear. What caused the children of Israel to lose faith? (v. 28)

Was their perception of the enemy based on fear or faith?

What was the correct perception of the enemy?

They were literally commanded, "Do not be terrified, or afraid of them" (v. 29). As believers in Jesus Christ, we should have the same mind-set of complete faith and not fear. What does 2 Timothy 1:7 tell us about the nature of fear?

According to 2 Timothy 1:7 list the three things God has given instead of a "spirit of fear."

1.

2.

3.

In Deuteronomy 2:25 we see the power of God's mighty covenant at work. Not only would the Israelites not have fear in their minds, but instead, the fear of them would be placed upon their enemies. Verse 25 states, "This day I will begin to put the dread and fear of you upon the nations under the whole heaven, who shall hear the report of you, and shall tremble and be in anguish because of you." This promise of having your enemies fear you is restated a number of times in the Bible. What does Deuteronomy 28:7 say that God will do to our enemies?

What will happen to our enemies if they "come out against us"?

After reading the above scriptures relating to fear being sent upon the enemies of God's people, explain how God's covenant caused this to happen. Specifically, what did God's people have to do in order for this powerful covenant to be activated?

In Deuteronomy 3:22 a command not to fear one's enemies is again restated: "You must not fear them, for the LORD your God Himself fights for you." What is the main reason we can be confident in the face of opposition and adversity when we are under attack?

Deuteronomy 4:1–8 records the great secret of power and success for all God's people. What is the the key to this success? (v. 1)

What two things are we specifically commanded regarding the Word of God? (v. 2)

1.

2.

Explain in your own words how you can diminish or dilute the power of God's Word by adding or taking from it.

What are we to be careful to observe? (vv. 5, 6)

What will be the results of our observing God's Word? (v. 6)

What will people say when we obey God's Word? (v. 6)

What great privileges that God's people have are discussed? (vv. 7, 8)

According to these scriptures, write down some examples of the responses of people when they see supernatural wisdom manifest among God's people?

How will this acknowledgment of the wisdom of God's people produce evangelism in our time?

Read Daniel 2:46–49 and write down how this principle was at work in Daniel's life.

What is the relationship between Deuteronomy 4:7 and Jeremiah 33:3, which says, "Call to Me, and I will answer you, and show you great and mighty things, which you do not know"?

Write down three ways you can apply Deuteronomy 4:7 and Jeremiah 33:3 to your life right now.

1.

2.

3.

In Deuteronomy 4:30, 31 Moses gives a prophetic word to the people regarding the latter days. In verse 27 Moses talks about the fact that the Jews would be scattered among the nations. Then in verses 30 and 31 he says, "When you are in distress, and all these things come upon you in the latter days, when you turn to the LORD your God and obey His voice (for the LORD your God *is* a merciful God), He will not forsake you nor destroy you, nor forget the covenant of your fathers which He swore to them." Since 1 Corinthians 10:11 states, "Now all these things happened to them as examples, and they were written for our admonition, upon whom the ends of the ages have come," what should we do as believers in Jesus Christ living in the midst of a world that is self-destructing? What privilege does verse 30 give us for what the Bible calls "the latter days"?

 FAITH ALIVE

Numbers 4:40 gives us a special promise: "You shall therefore keep His statutes and His commandments which I command you today, that it may go well with you and with your children after you, and that you may prolong your days in the land which the LORD your God is giving you for all time."

After studying this promise, apply it to your life and the lives of your family members in our world today. Write down seven ways obeying God's Word and His covenant can have positive effects.

1.

2.

3.

4.

5.

6.

7.

Lesson 12/Moses' Second Message
(Deut. 4:44—26:19)

UNDERSTANDING THE TEN COMMANDMENTS
(Deuteronomy 4:44—13:18)

The Ten Commandments have been the moral foundation of western civilization until very recently. The Ten Commandments codify many of the requirements of God's covenant with the children of Israel. Moses warns the children of Israel to obey the Ten Commandments and other instructions from God. Their obedience to the covenant would mean their total freedom and deliverance. The Ten Commandments were not restrictive. On the contrary, they produced power in the lives of the children of Israel. The covenant of God is the way back to Paradise. Adam and Eve lost Paradise when they disobeyed God in the Garden of Eden. Read Deuteronomy 5:1–22.

 FAITH ALIVE

Looking at the Ten Commandments, it is important not to see them as a list of "don'ts," but rather as a set of protective guidelines that enhance life. In the exercise below, write out the Ten Commandments in your own words in the left-hand column. In the right-hand column, write down in a short statement what positive results obedience to that commandment will produce. The goal is to perceive the Ten Commandments in their proper perspective as life-enhancers and not as restrictive instructions (Deut. 5:6–21).

Commandment	Positive Result of Obedience
1.	
2.	
3.	
4.	
5.	
6.	
7.	
8.	
9.	
10.	

Now let us examine the Ten Commandments in more detail. Deuteronomy 5:6, 7 states, "I am the LORD your God who brought you out of the land of Egypt, out of the house of bondage. You shall have no other gods before Me." For the believer in Jesus Christ, how does Egypt and the "house of bondage" represent our old life under the dominion of sin and Satan?

Verse 7 warns us not to have any other gods but God. List some other gods of our culture.

Deuteronomy 5:11 states, "You shall not take the name of the LORD your God in vain, for the LORD will not hold *him* guiltless who takes His name in vain." In our society, taking the Lord's name in vain with profanity is commonplace in films and television.

How does taking the Lord's name in vain actually increase spiritual darkness?

What detrimental effect does it cause in men's hearts?

What can believers do in terms of speaking God's name in thankfulness, praise, and worship to counteract the negative effect of taking the Lord's name in vain?

Verse 12 reminds us to "observe the Sabbath day, to keep it holy." How does violating a day of rest spiritually, psychologically, and physically harm the individual and society?

Stress is one of the main factors contributing to sickness and disease in our society. How could observation of the Sabbath help solve this stress problem?

What is the promise God gives to those who honor their father and mother? (v. 16)

Why do you think honoring our father and mother is a priority with God?

What does God think about the value and worth of each human life? (v. 17)

In light of this commandment how do you feel about both abortion and euthanasia?

Verse 18 states, "You shall not commit adultery." What does the violation of this commandment produce in lives of family members who are affected by this sin?

What is the ripple effect in society produced by marital unfaithfulness?

Verse 19 states, "You shall not steal." How would obedience to this commandment affect our major cities? Why do you think this commandment is not taken seriously by a lot of people?

Verse 21 states, "You shall not covet your neighbor's wife; and you shall not desire your neighbor's house, his field, his male servant, his female servant, his ox, his donkey, or anything that *is* your neighbor's." This commandment strikes right at the root of our consumeristic and materialistic society, which screams at us "New!" "Bigger!" "Better!" Tragically, this consumer mind-set affects even the way we relate to people and treat them as disposable items. It is important that we fully understand what being *covetous* means. In 1 Corinthians 6:10 the apostle Paul says, "nor thieves, nor <u>covetous,</u> nor drunkards, nor revilers, nor extortioners will inherit the kingdom of God."

 WORD WEALTH

Covetous, *pleonektes.* Literally "to have more." This word regresses from good to bad. *Pleon* is the basic word for more in quantity, quality, and number. *Pleonazo* means to do more, make more, or increase. *Pleonekteo* means to overreach. *Pleonexia* is avarice. *Pleonektes* means a greedy covetousness so eager for gain that it will defraud others. A person consumed with *pleonektes* will violate laws for unlawful gain. He will cunningly forge ahead at others' expense. Ephesians 5:3 tells us that covetousness is idolatry. Idolatry is an aggravated form of self-love motivated by ego-drive.[1]

From the above definition, it is clear that the reason that God warns us not to covet in the Ten Commandments is that covetousness violates the law of love, and God is love. In Ephesians 5:20 the apostle Paul gives us instructions on how to keep ourselves free from covetousness. Briefly explain how obeying this principle will keep you free from covetousness.

In Deuteronomy 6:4, 5 we read about the greatest commandment. "Hear, O Israel: The LORD our God, the LORD *is* one! You shall love the LORD your God with all your heart, with all your soul, and with all your strength."

   WORD WEALTH

One, *'echad*. One, a unit; united; unity. *'Echad* comes from the root *'achad*, "to bring together, to unify; to collect one's thoughts." *'Echad* serves to portray the same range of meaning as "one" does in English, from the very narrowest sense (one and one only, as in Eccl. 9:18, "one sinner destroys much good") to the broadest sense (one made up of many, as in Gen. 2:24, where a man and his wife "shall become one flesh"). Deuteronomy 6:4–6 is the most important text in the Old Testament. Jesus called it the greatest commandment of Scripture, and it remains the central confession of Judaism to the day. The foundational truth for world redemption is that there is one God who creates and redeems, and yet the New Testament shows that God is Father, Son, and Holy Spirit. Compare the unity of God to the unity of man made in His image: man is comprised of spirit, soul, and body (1 Thess. 5:23). Man is not three "beings" but "one being" with physical, emotional, and spiritual elements.[2]

After studying the above "Word Wealth," briefly explain why Deuteronomy 6:4–6 is considered the most important text in the Old Testament.

Study Deuteronomy 6:4–9. Why should God's commandments be diligently taught to children?

Why did God want the Israelites constantly to talk about the commandments during all their activities?

What did God mean when He said, "You shall bind them [His commandments] as a sign on your hand, and they shall be as frontlets between your eyes"? (v. 8)

Why did God command the Israelites in verse 9, "You shall write them [His commandments] on the doorposts of your house and on your gates"?

Deuteronomy 6:10 and 11 illustrates a powerful principle from the Word of God. On what basis did God promise to bless the children of Israel? (v. 10)

What was the common characteristic of the cities, houses, hewn-out wells, vineyards, and olive trees that God promised to give them? (vv. 10, 11)

Deuteronomy 6:17–25 gives us an outline of the covenant God made between Himself and the children of Israel. What is the key to keeping this covenant? (v. 17)

What is one of the results of this obedience to the Word of God? (v. 19)

Take a few a minutes to meditate on verses 17–19 and allow this Old Testament promise to speak to the situations in your life today. How can this biblical principle be applied to your life?

What should be the result of such obedience?

What are some of the "enemies" God will drive out of our lives if we obey and do what the Word of God says?

Read Deuteronomy 7:1 and compare it with Luke 11:26 where Jesus says, "Then he goes and takes with *him* seven other spirits more wicked than himself, and they enter and dwell there; and the last *state* of that man is worse than the first."

How many nations were listed in God's promise in Deuteronomy 7:1?

What is the number of spirits mentioned in Luke 11:26?

 BIBLE EXTRA

In both the Old Testament and New Testament Scriptures, God promises to drive out the enemy. Interestingly enough, the Hebrew word for Hittite is *Chittiy* which comes from the word *cheth*, which means *terror*. Also, *cheth* is related to the word for an aboriginal Canaanite which was another enemy nation. Both of these nations have names that mean "fear" in Hebrew.

To the New Testament believer in Jesus Christ, God promises deliverance out of the bondage of enemy spirits that are in rebellion from God. It is not by accident that 2 Timothy 1:7 says, "For God has not given us a <u>spirit of fear</u>, but of power and of love and of a sound mind." What does the New Testament covenant promise the believer in Jesus Christ regarding driving the enemy out of our Promised Land?

Beginning with Deuteronomy 7:12 Moses outlines the many blessings God has promised for obedience. Listed below are some of these blessings. In the space provided, write down next to the blessings some specific areas in your life where God has demonstrated His goodness toward you.

(v. 13) God will love you.

(v. 13) God will multiply you.

(v. 13) God will bless the fruit of your womb (children).

(v. 13) God will bless the fruit of your land (work).

(v. 13) God will bless your grain, new wine, oil, the increase of your cattle, and the offspring of your flock (every good thing you put your energy and time into, if He directs it).

(v. 14) God will bless you above all people and take away infertility from your life. Your bodies will be fruitful with children, and your entire lives will be fruitful. (Perhaps the example you use may deal with fruitfulness in your relationships or spiritual life or other areas.)

Read Psalm 1:1–3 and compare it with Deuteronomy 7:12–14. What is the similarity between the promises in these verses?

What is the condition for experiencing fruitfulness in life? (Deut. 7:12)

Deuteronomy 7:15 says, "And the LORD will take away from you all sickness, and will afflict you with none of the terrible diseases of Egypt which you have known, but will lay *them* on all those who hate you." Although this was a promise made to the children of Israel, look up Matthew 4:23 and answer the question, How does this promise affect believers in Jesus Christ who have a better covenant?

Deuteronomy 8:1 gives us the condition of possessing the land. What is this condition?

Study Deuteronomy 8:1–18, and explain the central theme of these verses of Scripture.

Verses 2 and 3 tell us that God humbled the children of Israel. What was the purpose of this humbling process? (v. 16)

The second half of verse 3 states, "That He might make you know that man shall not live by bread alone; but man lives by every *word* that proceeds from the mouth of the LORD." This is an important truth to grasp, that we live by the word that proceeds from the mouth of the Lord. "The obvious message of the passage is that there is no survival of the soul without God's Word—daily. . . . Israel's receiving the daily supply of manna makes clear that a regular, daily portion of God's Word is to be sought and fed upon by the believer. This is not a matter of legal duty, determining one's salvation, but a matter of personal responsibility, determining one's obedience to the pathway of discipleship. However, let no one suppose spiritual survival is possible for long without nourishment from the Word of God. First Peter 2:2 declares that God's Word is as essential to the believer as milk is to the newborn child. But as we come to terms with His Word as key to our survival, let us also see that God has given its pleasantness as a joyful source of sweetness for our living (Ps. 19:10)."[3]

Deuteronomy 8:12–14 reveals the unfortunate truth that when men and women prosper they can be tempted to turn their backs on God. In a very real sense, these verses explain what has happened in parts of our world today. Yet God's purpose for humbling the Israelites in the wilderness was to test them so that He might do them "good in the end" (v. 16). After reading this verse of Scripture, answer the question, Is God against prospering His people?

What is God's true purpose in establishing His covenant? (v. 18)

Why does God give His people the power to get wealth? (v. 18)

WORD WEALTH

Power, *koach.* Vigor, strength, force, capacity, power, wealth, means, or substance. Generally the word means "capacity" or "ability," whether physical, mental, or spiritual. Here Moses informs Israel that it is God who gives them the "ability" (power, means, endurance, capacity) to obtain wealth, for material blessings are included in the promises to the patriarchs and their descendants. Moses strictly warns Israel in verse 17 not to falsely conclude that this capacity for success is an innate talent, but to humbly acknowledge that it is a God-given ability.[4]

Take a few moments to study Deuteronomy 9:1–5. What was the primary lesson that God was teaching them? (v. 5)

On what basis did the children of Israel inherit the Promised Land?

Look up what the apostle Paul said in Ephesians 2:8, 9. What is the primary principle at work here?

How is it similar to Deuteronomy 9:4, 5?

Deuteronomy 10:12 tells us the essence of the Law, which is to love God with all of our hearts. Deuteronomy 10:16 warns us: "Therefore circumcise the foreskin of your heart, and be stiff-necked no longer." How can we apply this truth to our lives today? How can we let the Holy Spirit circumcise our hearts?

Why do we need to come before the Lord regularly and allow Him to cut away the hardness of our human fleshly natures?

What is it about our human nature that makes the need for an ongoing circumcision of our hearts by the Spirit of God?

What is the relationship between spiritual revival and allowing the Spirit of God to circumcise our hearts?

Read Deuteronomy 11:1–32 and take special care to notice how love and obedience are rewarded. What does God set before us? (v. 26)

What happens if we obey the commandments? (v. 27)

What happens if we disobey the commandments? (v. 28)

On the basis of these verses, as well as additional New Testament truths, in your own words answer the question, Is "luck" or "chance" a factor in the prosperity and blessing of a believer's life?

What do these passages of Scripture tell us about the power that God has given us to choose a blessed or cursed life?

Is success, in terms of God's blessings on our marriages, relationships, businesses, and ministries, an accident?

Deuteronomy 11:13, 14 states, "And it shall be that if you earnestly obey My commandments which I command you today, to love the LORD your God and serve Him with all your heart and with all your soul, then I will give *you* the rain for your land in its season, the early rain and the latter rain, that you may gather in your grain, your new wine, and your oil." According to these passages of Scripture, is having adequate rain to harvest crops merely a matter of coincidence?

In addition to the relationship between God's people fulfilling the covenant and God's ability to prosper them with rain and good crops, could there be a prophetic message in this passage of Scripture?

Is there a relationship between the word "rain" and an outpouring of God's Holy Spirit?

Notice the terms "gather in your grain," "new wine," and "oil" (v. 14). In your own words explain how the covenant of God, in both the Old and New Testaments, affects revival and the outpouring of God's Spirit upon humankind.

What is the significance of the following words?

Grain (John 4:35)

New Wine (Matt. 9:17)

Oil (Ex. 25:6)

Again, Deuteronomy 11:19–21 shows that God prioritizes teaching children the commandments and ways of God. Verse 19 states, "You shall teach them to your children, speaking of them when you sit in your house, when you walk by the way, when you lie down, and when you rise up." Verse 21 outlines a promise that is given to those who obey verse 19. What is that promise?

Deuteronomy 12:8 states, "You shall not at all do as we are doing here today—every man doing what *is* right in his own eyes." How does this verse describe the result of modern humanism in our society?

Deuteronomy 12:8 gives a definition of what is now termed "situational ethics" or "relative morality." Yet God gives people His Law and commandments in which to guide people in terms of ethics and morality. Describe why situational ethics or "every man doing whatever *is* right in his own eyes" cannot work.

Deuteronomy 12:29, 30 gives a powerful warning to the modern believer not to be seduced by the false values of the world system all around us. As Christians we are going against the flow of society because we have chosen to serve God and not self. How would you apply the truths of verse 30 in your own life?

What would some of the gods of our day be, and how can we avoid serving them?

Deuteronomy 13:1–8 warns the children of God about false prophets and false teachers and gives us a test to determine whether or not a prophet, sign, or wonder is from God.

What warning are we given about false signs and wonders? (vv. 1–3)

On the basis of Deuteronomy 13:2, how can we judge if a sign or wonder is from God?

According to verse 2, a false prophet with false signs and wonders will say, "Let us go after other gods." In other words, he or she will point to another god besides Jesus Christ. Read 1 John 4:1–6 and write down how we can discern the difference between the spirit of truth and the spirit of error.

The Bible speaks very strongly about prophets and dreamers who try to lead people away from serving the true God (v. 5). Yet God has not left us in the dark regarding spiritual discernment. The Bible is our true test regarding the legitimacy of any spiritual teaching. Ultimately, people are deceived because they do not read their Bible. Reading the Bible daily and becoming a member of a local church body of believers is the greatest protection against spiritual deception. In John 8:32, Jesus Christ said, "And you shall know the truth, and the truth shall make you free."

THE LAWS OF LIBERATION
(Deuteronomy 14:1—21:9)

Deuteronomy 14:22–29 teaches the principle of tithing. Verses 22 and 23 state, "You shall truly tithe all the increase of your grain that the field produces year by year. And you shall eat before the LORD your God, in the place where He chooses to make His name abide, the tithe of your grain and your new wine and your oil, of the firstborn of your herds and your flocks, that you may learn to fear the LORD your God always."

Verse 29 gives a promise to God's people who are obedient in their tithes: "that the LORD your God may bless you in all the work of your hand which you do." On the basis of verse

29, do we have a right to expect God's blessing when we are faithful to support God's work with our tithe?

 FAITH ALIVE

Read Malachi 3:8–12 and consider how tithing and giving offerings to God can insure that our own needs will be met. In this passage God promises to rebuke the devourer for our sakes. Write down five areas in your own life where the devourer may have come. How will tithing and giving offerings release God to rebuke the devourer in that area of your life?

1.

2.

3.

4.

5.

Deuteronomy 15:1–6 explains the biblical principle of releasing debts every seven years. Unlike societies that deal with debts through bankruptcy, inflation, and recession, the ancient Hebrew society dealt with debt reduction in a far more humane and efficient manner. Notice verse 4, which says, ". . . except when there may be no poor among you; for the LORD will greatly bless you in the land which the LORD your God is giving you to possess *as* an inheritance."

What was the condition of Moses' statement, "when there may be no poor among you"?

What promise does God give the children of Israel regarding borrowing money? (v. 6)

How does this affect believers in Jesus Christ in our contemporary society where borrowing is sometimes an economic necessity?

Deuteronomy 15:7, 8 reveals what our attitude should be toward the poor. Explain what our response to the poor should be.

 AT A GLANCE

THE JEWISH CALENDAR[5]				

The Jews used two kinds of calendars:
Civil Calendar—official calendar of kings, childbirth, and contracts.
Sacred Calendar—from which festivals were computed.

Names of Months	Corresponds with	No. of Days	Month of Civil Year	Month of Sacred Year
Tishri	Sept.–Oct.	30	1st	7th
Heshvan	Oct.–Nov.	29 or 30	2nd	8th
Chislev	Nov.–Dec.	29 or 30	3rd	9th
Tebeth	Dec.–Jan.	29	4th	10th
Shebat	Jan.–Feb.	30	5th	11th
Adar	Feb.–Mar.	29 or 30	6th	12th
Nisan	Mar.–Apr.	29 or 30	7th	1st
Iyar	Apr.–May	29	8th	2nd
Sivan	May–June	30	9th	3rd
Tammuz	June–July	29	10th	4th
Ab	July–Aug.	30	11th	5th
*Elul	Aug.–Sept.	29	12th	6th

*Hebrew months were alternately 30 and 29 days long. Their year, shorter than ours, had 354 days. Therefore, about every 3 years (7 times in 19 years) an extra 29-day month, Veadar, was added between Adar and Nisan.

Deuteronomy 16:1–6 gives instructions to celebrate the Passover. The Passover was a celebration of the Israelites' deliverance from bondage and slavery in Egypt. The Passover ceremony reminded the children of Israel that it was the fulfillment of God's covenant that brought them freedom. The eating of unleavened bread, or the bread of affliction, was symbolic of the hardships of Egypt and their slavery under Pharaoh (16:3). Eating of unleavened bread was supposed to remind them of what?

Deuteronomy 16:18–20 reveals to us God's order of justice. What is the essential aspect of God's requirement for them regarding legal matters?

Deuteronomy 17:14–20 gives principles to be used by governing kings. Israel was a theocratic state, where God was her only King. However, Moses prophesied that they would want human kings like the nations around them. Israel's kings would be expected to adhere to a strict set of disciplines. How does this passage make a commentary on spiritual leadership today?

Many of the scandals involving spiritual leadership of our time stem from pride, lust, and materialism. How could adherence to principles in Deuteronomy 17 keep someone from falling?

Deuteronomy 18:9–14 gives a strong warning against occult involvement. The children of Israel were warned to avoid the wicked customs of the culture that surrounded them. Believers in Jesus Christ should also avoid the wicked customs of our culture. What do these verses tell us about witchcraft, soothsaying, divination, omens, sorcery, spells, mediums (channeling), spiritists, communicating with the dead, and the like?

Can Christianity ever be mixed with these practices?

Deuteronomy 20:1–4 tells us not to be afraid of our enemies. Verse 1 states, "Do not be afraid," and verse 3 states, "Do not let your heart faint, do not be afraid, and do not tremble or be terrified because of them." What does this passage teach us about the things or people that oppose us in life? What does it teach us about spiritual warfare?

Read Zechariah 4:6 along with the above passages and give a short explanation of the central truth that God is trying to teach us involving all battles in life.

Deuteronomy 22:13–30 gives us laws of sexual morality. What do these passages of Scripture tell the believer in Jesus Christ about God's requirement of sexual purity? How does compromise of sexual purity erode God's power in our lives?

Deuteronomy 26:1–19 explains the relationship between tithes, offerings, and inheriting the promises of God. Obeying God's order of giving releases blessing in other areas. Verse 19 gives us a special promise when it says, "And that He will set you on high above all the nations which He has made, in praise, in name, and in honor, and that you may be a holy people to the LORD your God, just as He has spoken." How could this promise apply to the believer in Jesus Christ?

PROBING THE DEPTHS

In his book *A MAN'S IMAGE AND IDENTITY—A Study in a Man's Pathway to Christ-likeness in Today's Society,* Dr. Jack W. Hayford discusses what he terms the "Destruction Mandate." Dr. Hayford talks about how we are all made in the image of God. When we allow the Word of God to determine our perceptions of ourselves, our world and others, we find our true identities. Conversely, Dr. Hayford warns of the dangers of *idolatry,* which he defines as "the substituting of an alternate image (or 'circuit') for God's image . . . in our lives."[6]

Deuteronomy 7:1, 5, 6 states, "When the LORD your God brings you into the land which you go to possess, and has cast out many nations before you. . . . thus you shall deal with them: you shall destroy their altars, and break down their *sacred* pillars, and cut down their wooden images and burn their carved images with fire. For you are a holy people to the LORD your God; the LORD your God has chosen you to be a people for Himself, a special treasure above all the peoples on the face of the earth."

Commenting on the above scripture Dr. Hayford writes, "These few words from the longer passage of the Lord's command to Israel are as important to us today as to them when they entered the Canaanitish culture to conquer it. The 'No Covenant-No Mercy' mandate (Deut. 7:2) sounds so brutal we are tempted to rise in defense of those things before which God Almighty was so biting in His absolute commands. But a full reading of the text brings us to these words:

> "Therefore know that the Lord your God, He is God, the faithful God who keeps covenant and mercy for a thousand generations with those who love Him and keep His commandments."

Dr. Hayford continues, "Let us be strongly reminded that God's call to destroy the images which His people encountered was motivated by His knowledge that if they didn't, those images would eventually destroy them! Hear it, please: God's 'No Mercy' clause is an expression of His mercifulness! And when we grasp that, we'll understand all the more what horrific impact there is in the world's image system."[7]

Dr. Hayford urges you to take action and asks the question, "Where in your life do you need to allow God's Spirit to deal with such matters and to mold you into one who resists any facet of the world's image?" Briefly write down areas in your life in which you need to replace the inner images created by this world with the images formed by God's Word.

1. *Spirit-Filled Life Bible* (Nashville, TN: Thomas Nelson Publishers, 1991), 1726, "Word Wealth: 6:10 covetous."

2. Ibid., 263, "Word Wealth: 6:4 one."

3. Ibid., 266, "Kingdom Dynamics: God's Word and Our Soul's Nourishment."

4. Ibid., 267, "Word Wealth: 8:18 power."

5. Ibid., 276, Chart: "The Jewish Calendar."

6. Jack W. Hayford, *A Man's Image and Identity—A Study in a Man's Pathway to Christ-likeness in Today's Society* (Van Nuys, CA: Living Way Ministries, 1993).

7. Ibid.

Lesson 13/Moses' Third Message
(Deut. 27:1—30:20)

Deuteronomy 27:1—30:20 gives Moses' third message and contains one of my favorite chapters in the Bible, which is Deuteronomy 28. While many try to spiritualize Deuteronomy 28, the chapter contains a list of comprehensive blessings or curses to those who choose to obey or disobey God. In our culture which believes in chance, luck, or even things like random weather patterns, it is interesting to note the scope of conditions that God's covenant covers.

For example, bad weather and the crop failure or devastation it produces is not seen as the result of chance or mere atmospheric conditions. God's covenant actually promises good weather conditions to a nation that chooses to honor Him as God and follow His ways. In contrast, a nation or people that willfully ignore God and choose to violate His covenant can expect God to remove His hand of protection on the weather. Deuteronomy 28:12 states, "The LORD will open to you His good treasure, the heavens, to give rain to your land in its season." In Deuteronomy 28:24 we read, "The LORD will change the rain of your land to powder and dust; from the heaven it shall come down on you until you are destroyed."

Deuteronomy 27:1—30:20 contains the practical manifestations of God's supernatural covenant in all the affairs of life. In reading these chapters, it is important to grasp the truth that God's Word deals with all of life, not just some "religious" world. God is the God of the universe; and His covenant affects every single area of our lives. This was the central message that God was trying to teach Israel as they lived out their daily lives. It is also an important truth of what

God wants us to understand today. God is concerned about every area of our lives, and it is His desire to bless us.

THE LAW INSCRIBED ON STONES
(Deuteronomy 27:1–26)

The law is inscribed on stones. The people are reminded to obey it completely. Blessing is promised for obedience. Curses are promised to those who disobey. Specific sins that bring about a curse are given in Deuteronomy 27:15–26. List below ten sins that bring curses, described in the above verses.

1.

2.

3.

4.

5.

6.

7.

8.

9.

10.

Deuteronomy 28:1–68 describes some of the most powerful blessings in the Bible that are part of God's covenant. The condition for receiving them is that we must diligently obey the Word of God. It is important to understand that these promises were not just given to the children of Israel. These promises of blessing are given to believers in Jesus Christ if they obey God's Word and listen to His voice. These blessings cover every aspect of our lives: our children, our resources, our bank accounts, our relationships, our enemies, our ability to lend and not borrow—every area of life. Conversely, if we choose to disobey God's commandments and principles, then many facets of our lives will be cursed. It's not that God is sitting upon His throne giving us divine brownie points if we do good and zinging thunderbolts if we are bad. When we obey God's Word, His covenant is activated on our behalf. Kingdom principles and divine laws go into effect that can either benefit us or hurt us. These laws and principles are at work on physical, psychological, spiritual, and economic levels.

Study Deuteronomy 28:1–14, first focusing on verses 1 and 2: "Now it shall come to pass, if you diligently obey the voice of the LORD your God, to observe carefully all His commandments which I command you today, that the LORD your God will set you high above all nations of the earth."

After reading these two verses, it is clear that two of the operative terms are "diligently obey" and "carefully observe." Describe in your own words how these terms qualify the kind of obedience and observation of the Word of God that is needed to reap God's choicest blessings. Define the difference between this kind of obedience and a casual obedience to the Word of God.

Define what these terms mean to you living in contemporary society. In other words, translate these blessings to terms that are applicable to you. (For example, a blessing on your "storehouses" might translate to a "blessing on your bank account" or "investments." It is important to understand that these blessings were written in a language that spoke to an agricultural society. But God's covenant blessings still work just as powerfully in our high-tech society. Deuteronomy 28 is not a guarantee that we will have no problems in life or that we will all become millionaires. However, it does speak powerfully to us that God will send us His favor and blessing, in both spiritual and material ways, if we are faithful to Him.)

(v. 3) "Blessed *shall* you *be* in the city, and blessed *shall* you *be* in the country."

(v. 4) "Blessed *shall be* the fruit of your body, the produce of your ground and the increase of your herds, the increase of your cattle and the offspring of your flocks."

(v. 5) "Blessed *shall be* your basket and your kneading bowl."

(v. 6) "Blessed *shall* you *be* when you come in, and blessed *shall* you *be* when you go out."

(v. 7) "The LORD will cause your enemies who rise against you to be defeated before your face; they shall come out against you one way and flee before you seven ways."

(v. 8) "The LORD will command the blessing on you in your storehouses and in all to which you set your hand."

(v. 11) "And the LORD will grant you plenty of goods, in the fruit of your body, in the increase of your livestock, in the produce of your ground."

(v. 12) "The LORD will open to you His good treasure, the heavens, to give rain to your land in its season, and to bless all the work of your hand. You shall lend to many nations, but you shall not borrow."

(v. 13) "And the LORD will make you the head and not the tail; you shall be above only, and not beneath."

What are the conditions of these blessings? (v. 13)

What additional conditions were there regarding the Word of God and idolatry? (v. 14)

Deuteronomy 28:15–68 reviews the horrible consequences of disobeying the covenant of God. Basically, the curses outlined here are a complete reversal of the blessings. It is interesting to note that many of the consequences of disobedience could be read out of our morning newspapers as adverse sociological, weather, and economic factors. Could it be that our nation, which was once blessed so favorably by God, is now experiencing the result of what happens when God removes His hand of blessing? Read carefully and take note how things like adverse weather conditions, diseases and plagues, confusion in the inner cities, lack of vision, fear, foreigners buying up the land, and economic debt are directly related to the removal of God's blessing upon a nation.

Verse 15 gives us the primary reason that such curses can come upon an individual or nation. In your own words write down what that reason is.

What would happen if Israel did not serve the Lord with joy and gladness of heart? (vv. 47, 48)

What lesson does this teach us as believers in Jesus Christ? (Phil. 4:4)

Deuteronomy 29:1–29 is a review of the covenant. What was the central truth that God was communicating? (vv. 22–25)

God did not want anyone in the dark as to why bad things were happening in the land. Adverse weather, bad economic conditions, plagues, social unrest, and other negative happenings were a direct result to the people's disobedience of the covenant and the Word of God. How do verses 22–25 spell this out?

How does this contrast with what experts in our day say when they proclaim "these problems are very complex"?

Are our problems today as "complex" as the experts would say, or are many of our problems related to society's walking in ways that are contrary to God's laws of abundance, peace, and fruitfulness?

Deuteronomy 30:1–20 reviews the blessings of God. How is circumcision of our hearts essential to walking continually in the Lord's blessings? (v. 6)

What will happen if we as believers in Jesus Christ do not regularly allow the Holy Spirit and the Word of God to circumcise our hearts?

What in our human natures makes regular circumcision of the heart necessary?

Deuteronomy 30:11–15 calls us to accountability before God. Verse 11 says, "For this commandment which I command you today *is* not *too* mysterious for you, nor *is* it far off." According to verses 11–14, why is there no excuse for not obeying God's Word?

What is the key to walking in God's blessings? (v. 14)

How does this verse relate to Deuteronomy 11:18–20?

What is the principle that God is trying to establish concerning knowing His Word?

Finally, verse 15 gives us the crux of the matter, "See, I have set before you today life and good, death and evil." The idea is that we *choose* whether or not we will walk in blessing. Verse 19 repeats this message when it says, "I have set before you life and death, blessing and cursing; therefore choose life, that both you and your descendants may live." What does this scripture tell us about our responsibility in receiving God's blessings in our lives?

Lesson 14/Moses' Final Word and a New Leader
(Deut. 31:1—34:12)

Moses turns over the leadership of the children of Israel to Joshua. In addition, Moses delegates to the levitical priests and the elders the responsibility of teaching the Law, which was to be read every seven years. Moses warns Joshua of the future apostasy of the Israelites so that he will be aware of the danger and take steps to avert it. Finally, before Moses' death on Mount Nebo, he gives his final blessing on each of the tribes of Israel except Simeon, which became part of Judah. In chapter 32 we read the "Song of Moses," which warns Israel of God's judgment for her unfaithfulness. In chapter 33 Moses gives powerful prophetic blessings to the nation of Israel regarding her future glory and greatness. Finally, Moses dies at 120 years old and leaves Israel in the charge of Joshua who must lead them into the Land of Promise.

A CHANGE OF LEADERSHIP
(Deuteronomy 31:1–29)

In Deuteronomy 31:1–8, Joshua is selected as the new leader of Israel. The children of Israel are encouraged to be strong, of good courage, and not afraid. The theme of Deuteronomy 31:6 and 8 is repeated throughout the Bible. Look up Joshua 1:6, 7, and 9. List below the purpose of obeying the following commandments in the Christian walk.

1. Be strong.

2. Be of good courage.

3. Do not be afraid.

4. Do not fear.

5. Do not be dismayed.

Deuteronomy 31:9–13 tells us that the Law is to be read before all of Israel every seven years. Verse 13 reveals the purpose of reading the Law before all of Israel?

In Deuteronomy 31:14–29 God inaugurates Joshua into leadership. In verses 16 and 20 Moses gives a prophetic word regarding the future rebellion of the children of Israel. Yet God does not give up on Israel or the human race. What does this tell us about God's character? (See 2 Pet. 3:9.)

Deuteronomy 32:1–43 records the Song of Moses, which is both prophetic and instructional. It tells the story of God and His relationship with Israel. Deuteronomy 32:2 states, "Let My teaching drop as the rain, My speech distill as the dew, as raindrops on the tender herb, and as showers on the grass." What does this verse tell us about the importance of God's Word in our lives and in keeping the covenant?

Verse 13 says, "He made him ride in the heights of the earth." What is God's plan for our lives if we read and obey His Word? What should our attitude and expectation be when we obey God?

Too often, obedience to the Word of God is viewed as a solemn and legalistic discipline. The Song of Moses tells about the positive results of obedience to God's covenant. Review verses 10b, 11, 13, and 43. Write down what obeying God's Word can produce in your own life?

Conversely, review verses 23, 24, and 33. Disobeying the Word of God produces very negative results. It is important to remember that God is not sitting upon His throne waiting to "zap" people for being bad. However, the Song of Moses warns us about what can happen when the people of God deliberately walk out from under His divine covering of protection. Verses 24 and 33 make reference to the "teeth of beasts," "the poison of serpents," and the "venom of cobras." The Bible teaches us about the "serpent of old." How do these references to snakes (often a symbol for demons and Satan) tell us about how we can become the prey to demonic forces when we walk out from under God's covenant covering of protection?

What two things did God provide atonement for? (Deut. 32:43)

How did this atonement find its ultimate expression in Jesus Christ?

Deuteronomy 33:1 states, "Now this is the blessing with which Moses the man of God blessed the children of Israel before His death." Why were these final blessings of Moses so totally positive in light of the strong warnings regarding disobedience recorded in the previous chapter? What does this say about the character of God?

Deuteronomy 34:1–12 records Moses' death on Mount Nebo. The torch of leadership is passed on to Joshua in verse 9: "Now Joshua the son of Nun was full of the spirit of wisdom, for Moses laid his hands on him; so the children of Israel heeded him, and did as the LORD commanded Moses." What does this passage of scripture tell us about how God passes on His anointing for leadership to each new generation?

Read Deuteronomy 34:10–12. What do these two verses tell us about Moses and what God did through him?

How did Moses with all of his glory merely foreshadow the Savior to come, Jesus Christ?

The message of the gospel of Jesus Christ is that if we trust God and put our faith in Jesus Christ, then God can save us and give us eternal life, and He can also deliver us here on earth and miraculously provide. The central truth of the Old Testament (Old Covenant) is that if the children of God obey His Word and keep the covenant, then God will heal, save, and deliver. The message of the better covenant or New Testament is that it is our faith in Jesus Christ and His atonement for our sins that releases the flow of God's blessings in our lives, starting with eternal salvation and covering such earthly needs as healing, deliverance, provision, guidance, and sanctification.

AT A GLANCE

TRUTH-IN-ACTION through DEUTERONOMY[1]
Letting the LIFE of the Holy Spirit Bring Faith's Works Alive in You!

Truth Deuteronomy Teaches	Text	**Action** Deuteronomy Invites
1 Steps to Knowing God and His Ways Deut. focuses on how God brings His people to maturity. He will not allow us to skip any of the steps in the process and will make sure we complete it.	2:14 7:22 32:11, 12	**Know** that God will always bring you back to face any area of growth you have tried to skip. **Do not despise** small advances. The process toward maturity is made up mostly of small steps, rather than major ones. **Rest** in God's nurturing care. **Know** that He has committed Himself to care for you, guide you, and bring you to maturity.
2 Steps to Dynamic Devotion Deut. adds much to our understanding of being devoted to God with all of our heart and soul. It emphasizes the need for wholehearted commitment. God calls His people to pursue Him with all of their strength.	1:42 4:1, 2, 6–8 4:29; 6:4, 5	**Seek out** and **depend upon** God's presence. Without it, victory is unlikely, if not impossible. **Study** God's Word faithfully and carefully. **Apply** it to all you think and do. God will show His goodness and greatness. **Seek** God's face continually. **Do not neglect** prayer and Scripture meditation.
3 Steps to Holiness Holiness means being separated from and distinct from the world. Deut. gives much insight into the positive disciplines for building lives that are fully dedicated to God.	11:18–21 12:25, 28, 32 30:15–20	**Practice** Scripture memorization and meditation to fix God's Word in your consciousness and allow it to change your behavior. **Seek out** from the Scriptures the ways God wants you to live, and **practice them** so that your life will be pleasing to Him. **Understand** that when you choose any action, you choose its consequences as well. God cannot bless and prosper disobedience and unfaithfulness.
4 Guidelines for Growing in Godliness Deut. gives much attention to the practices that will help you live with a continual God-consciousness, making more and more room for Him in your	8:10–20	**Guard against** pride amid God's blessings. **Know** that prosperity often brings arrogance, causing us to forget that God is the source of all blessing.

life. Godly people are careful to maintain proper attitudes and disciplines in their relationships. Deut. also explores how to maintain a proper regard for the authority God's Word has in life and conduct.	12:4, 8, 13 13:1–5; 18:21, 22 21:18–21	**Measure** your conduct and attitudes regularly according to God's Word. **Test** all ministry by God's Word. **Reject** any ministry that does not measure up to the Bible. **Give attention** to proper parental discipline. Rebellious children bring shame to their parents and dishonor the Lord.
5 Steps to Dealing with Sin It is important to deal with sins of heart and attitude before they fester, poisoning our lives and resulting in hateful actions.	29:18 31:5–8 31:29	**Guard against** bitterness in your own heart and among God's people. It most often causes people to turn away from God. **Turn away** from fear, faint-heartedness, and discouragement. All unbelief is sin. **Trust** in God's presence. He promises to be with you always to keep you from fear. **Remain mindful** of your proneness to sin and turning away from God. **Acknowledge** and rely on God's strength and abundant provision.
6 Keys to Moral Purity Deut. reiterates that moral and sexual purity are essential to covenant loyalty to God. God's standards cannot be compromised and are usually in stark contrast to social standards of those among whom God's people dwell.	22:13–21 22:22	**Value** virginity; **do not be ashamed** of it. **Shun** today's casual attitude toward sexual relationships. **Realize** that God places a high premium on sexual purity. **Flee from** and **detest** adultery, and **honor** marital fidelity. **Understand** that God rejects adultery and will always judge it severely.
7 Guidelines to Gaining Victory Many scriptures point to our involvement in active spiritual combat, in which we must conduct ourselves as good soldiers. No wonder, then, that learning how to gain victory in this warfare is so important.	3:21, 22 30:11–14	**Remember,** the battle is the Lord's. **Trust** your battles to Him, and **rest** in His victory. He will fight for you. **Be confident** that God will supply the dynamic for all He demands. **Understand** that our life in Christ is a life of faith. **Depend** upon His constant provision.

1. *Spirit-Filled Life Bible* (Nashville, TN: Thomas Nelson Publishers, 1991), 302–303, "Truth-in-Action through Deuteronomy."